Penguin Handbooks

The Brecon Beacons National Park

Hugh Westacott was born in London in 1932 and moved to Epsom,
Surrey, on the outbreak of the war. He was educated at Tiffin Boys'
School, Kingston-upon-Thames, and the North-Western
Polytechnic. He was for ten years the Deputy County Librarian of
Buckinghamshire and has also worked as a librarian in Sutton,
Croydon, Sheffield, Bradford and Brookline, Massachusetts.
During the war he spent his holidays with his family in Colyton,
east Devon, walking five miles to the sea and back each day, and
his love of walking stems from these experiences. He is now a
freelance writer and lecturer and in 1979 he was commissioned by
Penguin to write this series of footpath guides to every national
park and official long-distance path. He has also written *The
Walker's Handbook* (Penguin, second edition 1980) and two
forthcoming books, *Long-Distance Paths: An International
Directory* and *The Backpacker's Bible*. His other interests include
the history of the Royal Navy in the eighteenth century and the
writings of Evelyn Waugh. Hugh Westacott is married and has two
daughters.

Mark Richards was born in 1949 in Chipping Norton, Oxfordshire.
He was educated at Burford Grammar School before training for a
farming career. He discovered the pleasures of hill walking through
a local mountaineering club. He became friends with Alfred
Wainwright, the creator of a unique series of pictorial guides to the
fells of northern England, who encouraged him to produce a guide
to the Cotswold Way, which was followed by guides to the North
Cornish Coast Path and Offa's Dyke Path. For two years he
produced a selection of hill walks for the *Climber and Rambler*
magazine, and more recently he has contributed articles and
illustrations to the *Great Outdoors* magazine and numerous walking
books, culminating in the present series of Penguin footpath
guides. As a member of various conservation organizations and a
voluntary warden of the Cotswolds Area of Outstanding Natural
Beauty, he is interested in communicating the need for the
protection of environmental and community characteristics,
particularly in rural areas. Mark Richards is happily married with
two lively children, Alison and Daniel.

The Penguin Footpath Guides

To be published:

Long-Distance Paths: An International Directory
The Cleveland Way
The Cornwall South Coast Path
The Cornwall North Coast Path
Exmoor National Park
The Lake District National Park
Northumberland National Park
The North York Moors National Park
Offa's Dyke Path
The Peak District National Park
The Pembrokeshire Coast National Park
The Pembrokeshire Coast Path
The Pennine Way
Snowdonia National Park
A Westmorland Way
The Yorkshire Dales National Park

Already published:

Dartmoor for Walkers and Riders
The Devon South Coast Path
The Dorset Coast Path
The North Downs Way
The Ridgeway Path
The Somerset and North Devon Coast Path
The South Downs Way

The Brecon Beacons National Park

H. D. Westacott

With maps by Mark Richards

Penguin Books

*For my nephew, Guy Matthews, with whom
I spent a happy weekend backpacking in the
Brecon Beacons in February 1979*

Penguin Books Ltd, Harmondsworth, Middlesex, England
Penguin Books, 625 Madison Avenue, New York, New York 10022, U.S.A.
Penguin Books Australia Ltd, Ringwood, Victoria, Australia
Penguin Books Canada Ltd, 2801 John Street, Markham, Ontario, Canada L3R 1B4
Penguin Books (N.Z.) Ltd, 182–190 Wairau Road, Auckland 10, New Zealand

First published 1983

Text copyright © H. D. Westacott, 1983
Maps copyright © Mark Richards, 1983
All rights reserved

Made and printed in Great Britain by
Richard Clay (The Chaucer Press) Ltd, Bungay, Suffolk
Set in Monophoto Univers

Contents

Contents

Acknowledgements

I should like to express my deep appreciation of the help given in the writing of this guide by the staff of the Brecon Beacons National Park. In particular, Mr Roger Stevens has been an unfailing source of help and has answered my numerous queries efficiently, promptly and with great courtesy.

Needless to say, the views expressed in the guide are my own and are not necessarily shared by the National Park Committee or its officers.

Mark Richards has not only drawn the superb maps but also given much valuable advice on the choice of routes and I am very grateful for his help. The maps are based on the 1:25000 Ordnance Survey maps, with the sanction of the Controller of Her Majesty's Stationery Office.

My thanks are due, too, to Sue Baylis for typing the manuscript.

Introduction

The best way to see and experience the glorious scenery of the Brecon Beacons National Park is by walking or riding in it. The most spectacular parts are remote from roads and cannot be seen by motorists who are not prepared to leave their cars behind. It is true that some of the roads pass through fine scenery with good views, but it is only those who are prepared to saddle their horse or pull on their boots who will see the best parts of this delectable landscape. Those who go at man's natural pace of two or two and a half miles per hour will feel the wind on their cheek and the blood coursing through their veins as they climb steadily and rhythmically to the mountain tops and they will see sights that they will recollect with joy and thankfulness for the rest of their lives.

The name Brecon Beacons is properly applied only to a small area to the south of Brecon, but the name has been given to the whole of the National Park. The Brecon Beacons National Park, established in 1957 under the provisions of the National Parks and Access to the Countryside Act of 1949, covers an area of 519 square miles. Much of the Park lies within the county of Powys, but its boundaries also include parts of Gwent, Dyfed and Mid-Glamorgan. It is administered by a committee made up of representatives of the constituent counties, together with other members appointed by the Secretary of State for Wales. The National Park Committee has the statutory duty of 'preserving and enhancing the natural beauty of the Park and the promotion of its enjoyment by the public'.

Visitors to the National Park should understand that such a designation in no way alters the ownership of the land. The nation does not own it and the land is not nationalized. Most of the farms are privately owned, and the land owned by the Forestry Commission and the Water Authority, although in a sense public property, is fenced and access is restricted. Persons using the National Park for recreation should remember that the whole of it, even the highest parts, is farmed and that sheep and ponies are likely to be found anywhere.

Introduction

The headquarters of the National Park are at Glamorgan Street, Brecon, Powys LD3 7DP, and there are Information Centres here and at:

Monk Street, Abergavenny, Gwent NP7 5NA
Broad Street, Llandovery, Dyfed SA20 0AR
Craig-y-nos Country Park, Pen-y-cae, Powys SA19 1GL
Danywenallt Study Centre, Talybont, Brecon, Powys LD3 7YS
Brecon Beacons Mountain Centre, Near Libanus, Brecon, Powys LD3 8ER

The Mountain Centre is particularly worth visiting as it is purpose-built and always has interesting exhibitions and displays.

All the Information Centres have collections of leaflets, maps and guides of interest to the visitor and the staff are enthusiasts and unfailingly helpful and courteous.

The purpose of this guide, one of a series covering each of Britain's National Parks, is to assist walkers and riders to explore the Brecon Beacons by using public rights of way and other recognized routes. Although written primarily for walkers, many of the routes are on bridleways and can be used by horse riders and pedal cyclists, although the grading system is applicable to walkers only. The routes vary in length from 3 miles to 17 miles and are graded so that there are some to appeal to all tastes, from the motorist who wants a half-day stroll, to the family walker who is content with 8 miles or so, or the hardened fell-walker who wants a full day in the mountains.

A great deal of thought has gone into the design and format of the guide in order to make it as easy to use as possible. Both the maps and the route descriptions are very detailed and always appear opposite each other, so that there is no need to be constantly turning the pages.

The maps

The maps in the guide are based on the 1:25000 (approximately 2½ ins. to the mile) Ordnance Survey maps updated and corrected by means of personal survey. Information not shown on the Ordnance Survey maps has been added, including the location of gates, stiles and signposts. A further refinement is that walls and fences or hedges are distinguished from each other. In order to keep the maps as legible as possible, contour lines have been omitted and hills and mountains are shown by tapered strokes, which give a very clear idea of the shape of the landscape and should be helpful to those who find contour lines difficult to interpret. The numbers shown on the line of the path refer to the paragraph numbers in the text, so that the map can be cross-referenced to the text. North is shown on the maps but it is not always at the top of the page. Grid lines are not shown on the maps themselves, but in the margins will be found the grid line numbers, allowing the maps in the guide to be used in conjunction with any edition of the Ordnance Survey map.

A problem faced by all writers of footpath guides is how to cope with maps that are too large to fit on to one page. Rather than adopt the traditional solution of adjusting the scale to fit the page, thus losing much essential detail and confusing the walker, a solution has been found by dividing the route into sections with a separate map for each one and with the route description opposite the map to which it refers. Wherever possible the maps have been drawn so that, with the guide held in a natural reading position, the route starts at the bottom of the page and runs upwards. The continuation of a route from one map to the next is indicated by the letters in the margin, A joining up with A, B with B and so on. In some instances the shape of the route requires that two separate sections of the walk should appear on one map and in these cases it will be necessary to turn back to the appropriate page. Instructions are also given in the route descriptions as well as in the margin of the maps. As north is indicated on all the maps it is easy to align the different sections.

Small-scale maps showing the different sections of the whole route are provided at the beginning of every route description. These maps give the walker an overall picture of the route, showing how the different sections fit together, and, to those unfamiliar with the area, are useful for locating the start of each route on a road map. Beneath these maps will be found a profile of the path which gives a very clear idea of how strenuous are the climbs. Distances in miles are shown on the path profile.

The route descriptions

Great care has been taken to describe the routes as precisely and as accurately as possible so that those who find maps something of a mystery may follow the path as readily as a competent map-reader. As far as possible the routes have been described in relation to objects and landmarks that are normally not subject to change, but it should be remembered that the countryside is always changing and the accuracy of a route description can be guaranteed only at the time that it is made. New buildings and fences can soon make the instructions out of date. *The words 'left', 'right' and 'forward' are always made with reference to the direction of travel.*

Occasionally paths are diverted from their original route. Whenever this occurs the National Park Department will indicate the new route by means of waymarks and signposts. Such diversions supersede the instructions in the guide.

Readers are urged to report all cases of obstruction to the Headquarters of the National Park, giving a brief description of the problem and its exact location, together with a grid reference.

The author would appreciate comments on any inaccuracies or ambiguities. These will be investigated and any changes incorporated in later editions and the source acknowledged. Address all communications to H. D. Westacott, c/o Penguin Books Ltd, 536 King's Road, London SW10 0UH.

At the beginning of every route description will be found basic information about public transport, parking and the availability of refreshments. Readers are urged to carry sufficient food and drink with them as it is unwise to rely on cafés and public houses, especially out of season.

Grading of routes

In order to assist the walker to choose routes within his walking ability the walks are graded according to the nature of the terrain and the degree of skill required to navigate the path.

Grading of the terrain

Easy: Short routes over well-defined paths and tracks usually avoiding mountainous country. There may be some short steep climbs, but all these walks should be suitable for the inexperienced in reasonable health.

Moderately difficult: Routes generally between 7 and 10 miles long over paths which may at times be indistinct but which follow clearly defined features such as walls, fences and streams. On some of these routes there may be stretches across mountainous country, but here the paths will be clearly defined. These routes are not suitable for those with no walking experience.

Difficult: These routes are generally, though not always, longer, and usually at least 8 miles in length. They often include considerable stretches of mountainous country, sometimes where no proper path exists and where the ground underfoot is likely to be broken, difficult and wet. These routes are suitable only for experienced mountain walkers.

Route-finding grades

Easy: Routes over well-defined paths and tracks. No map-reading skills are required and the walker should have no difficulty in following the path from the route description alone.

Moderately difficult: Routes over paths which may not always be visible on the ground and where it may be necessary to follow such features as walls, fences, streams and ridges.

Difficult: Routes in mountainous country where paths sometimes do not exist. Anyone using these routes must be skilled in the use of map and compass and always carry the 1:25000 or 1:50000 Ordnance Survey map. Compass bearings are sometimes given in those circumstances where no description will suffice.

Rights of way in the National Park

The National Park Committee is vested with statutory powers to assert and protect the interests of those who use public rights of way and, generally speaking, the officers carry out this duty very well. They have prepared a definitive map showing all public paths within the National Park and, as far as resources permit, these paths are maintained. Most paths appear to be recorded accurately on the definitive map and I know of only one instance, near Penderyn, where a public path is shown wrongly on the map.

There are a considerable number of well-used paths which appear neither on the definitive map nor on any edition of the Ordnance Survey map. For example, most of the long ridges of the Black Mountains have paths along the whole of their lengths. Presumably, when the next review of the definitive map takes place, these will be claimed.

The National Park divides its paths into two categories — priority paths and non-priority paths. Most of the budget assigned to maintaining the path network is spent on priority paths, as these are regarded as the more important routes for walkers and riders. On the more popular routes much remedial work has to be done to combat the effects of erosion caused by over-use, and it is easy to see why, in an era of financial stringency, it has been found necessary to implement a policy of regarding some paths as more important than others. It is to be hoped that the non-priority paths will not be forgotten entirely, as there are a number of potentially useful routes which cannot be used at present because they are obstructed and which, if they were opened up, would take some of the pressure off the well-used paths. Even in Mynydd Du forest in the Black Mountains, a well-walked area, there are a number of useful paths which appear to be unusable because they are blocked by the conifers planted by the Forestry Commission. A map showing the network of priority paths may be inspected at the Headquarters of the National Park in Brecon. Public rights of way are shown on the Outdoor Leisure Map of the Brecon Beacons published by the Ordnance Survey.

As part of its overall policy of path management, the National Park discourages the inclusion in footpath guides of routes in the area south of the Carmarthen Fans, near Llanddeusant, and north of Ystradgynlais. This is a very wild region with few rights of way. The terrain is very broken and difficult and should be explored only by experienced mountain walkers who are competent with map and compass.

Access to open country

It is only on public rights of way that walkers and riders have the legal right to explore the countryside, but within the National Park there is a tradition of general access to open country (those mountainous areas beyond the boundaries of fences, walls and hedges). Providing that they conduct themselves properly and unobtrusively walkers and riders are tolerated in open country and are unlikely to be challenged if they wander at will. There are only two areas of open country where access is expressly forbidden except on public paths: in the National Nature Reserve at Craig Cerrig-gleisiad (grid reference SN9422) just west of the A470, 2 miles north-west of the Storey Arms, and also in an area roughly bounded by Ystradfellte, Penwyllt, Cwm Newynydd and Heol Senni in Fforest Fawr. There is a rifle range used by the army about 2 miles north of Pen y Fan on the edge of the open country south of Brecon. The boundaries are clearly marked with posts and walkers are unlikely to blunder into it by accident.

Public transport

Public transport services throughout the National Park are poor. There are train services to Abergavenny from Paddington, Cardiff and Newport, and Llandeilo, Llangadog, Llanwrda and Llandovery are served by the Central Wales line from Llanelli to Shrewsbury.

Bus services tend to follow the main roads and there are considerable areas of the National Park which have no services at all. Many of the routes in this guide are remote from bus services.

The Development Board for Rural Wales, Ladywell House, Newtown, Powys SY16 1JB, tel. (0868) 26965, publish a train and bus timetable for mid-Wales which includes the Brecon Beacons National Park. (At least one edition of this timetable was not complete as claimed and the index was poor and difficult to use.)

Another timetable is published by the National Welsh Omnibus Services Ltd, 253 Cowbridge Road West, Ely, Cardiff CG5 5XX, tel. (0222) 591371. The Area 2 edition (Gwent and Rhymney Valleys and Merthyr Tydfil) includes all bus services in the National Park except those run by independent operators.

Information about bus services may also be obtained from The Bus Station and Travel Office, Monmouth Road, Abergavenny, Gwent, tel. (0873) 3249.

What to wear

During the summer months the only requirements for the easy and moderately difficult routes in settled weather are stout shoes, a plastic or nylon raincoat, a rucksack for carrying food and drink and spare sweaters (it is always much colder on the tops and ridges). A plastic bag is useful for protecting this guide from the elements.

Those undertaking the difficult routes should be properly equipped for mountain walking with boots, cagoule and over-trousers, first-aid kit, compass and Ordnance Survey map, survival bag and whistle, food, drink and spare clothing and a rucksack to contain them all. For winter wear, see p. 19.

Maps and the compass

The Ordnance Survey publish an Outdoor Leisure Map in 3 sheets covering the whole of the National Park based on the first series edition of the 1:25000 map. These maps show public rights of way and should be purchased by anyone planning to do some serious walking in the area. The scale is approximately $2\frac{1}{2}$ ins. to the mile.

The 1:50000 map (approximately $1\frac{1}{4}$ miles to the inch) also shows rights of way, but the smaller scale precludes the inclusion of much of the detail shown on the Outdoor Leisure Map. Sheets 159, 160 and 161 of the Landranger edition of the 1:50000 map between them cover the whole of the National Park.

All walkers planning to undertake the difficult or moderately difficult routes in this guide should carry with them the relevant Ordnance Survey map and a compass *and know how to use them*. They will be found invaluable for setting the maps in the guide in the context of the surrounding countryside. Should the weather suddenly deteriorate they will be useful for finding escape routes to lower ground.

In a few cases where it is not possible to describe the route clearly, compass bearings have been given. Readers should note that all such bearings are *magnetic* and were correct in 1980. The bearing *decreases by* $\frac{1}{2}°$ every 4 years.

Hazards and dangers

All mountainous areas must be treated with great respect and the rules of mountain safety should always be obeyed. In summer the main dangers are getting lost and being disorientated by the sudden descent of mist and low cloud. Nobody who has not actually experienced this phenomenon can have any idea how frightening it can be. All sense of direction is lost and unless following a clearly defined path the walker is likely to go round and round in circles. A further hazard in a mist is the risk of walking over the edge of some of the precipitous mountainsides.

It is important to carry adequate foul-weather clothing and warm sweaters. Even in summer it is possible to suffer from exposure if there is a strong wind and the walker is soaked to the skin. This condition is not readily recognized, but it can lead to collapse, and eventually death, in a relatively short time.

In winter the dangers are immeasurably greater and in recent years a number of members of the crack SAS Brigade have succumbed while conducting expeditions in blizzard conditions.

These words of advice are not intended to discourage prudent walkers from enjoying the mountains but are intended only as a warning not to attempt routes beyond their abilities or in unsuitable conditions. It is always a good plan to tell some responsible person of your route *and to notify them when you have returned*. This is important to prevent a fruitless search by the Mountain Rescue Team.

The weather

Like all mountainous areas in Wales, the Brecon Beacons National Park seems to get more than its fair share of rain. The prevailing south-westerly winds bring wet weather in from the Atlantic and the mountain tops are often covered with mist and low cloud. In such conditions, dedicated walkers who are determined to walk in all conditions should consider following some of the lowland routes in the waterfall country (see routes 6, 7 and 8).

South Wales is generally mild, even in winter, but remember that the temperature on the tops is certain to be considerably lower than in the valleys. In still air the temperature falls by 1°F for every 300 ft climbed, and as the wind is always very much stronger on the exposed ridges and mountain tops it is essential to carry extra sweaters even on the warmest days.

In winter the area is sometimes subject to severe blizzards. Although the snow does not generally lie for long in the valleys it can persist for long periods on the high ground.

A local weather forecast may be obtained by telephoning Cardiff (0222) 8091.

Mountain rescue

Mountain rescue services are co-ordinated by the police. Their task will be made much easier and the rescue effected more quickly if a little forethought is exercised. Providing that the patient is not suffering from serious injuries it is a good plan to move him to a sheltered spot to protect him from the wind and rain. Make a careful note of his exact position on the map and work out the grid reference. Take a note of his name and address and the nature of any injuries. Protect him as much as possible from the cold by putting over him all the clothing that can be spared. If possible, leave someone with him and then work out the quickest way of getting help. If there is no farm nearby it is probably best to go to the nearest road and flag down a car to take you to the nearest telephone. Dial 999 and give the police all the information you have collected. Listen very carefully to their instructions and do exactly what they tell you. Remember that it can take several hours to call out and gather together the voluntary members of the Mountain Rescue Team from their places of work.

It is important to maintain the morale of the patient by comforting words and an air of confidence and cheerfulness. An injured person can derive much comfort from physical contact with another person.

Walking in winter

Experienced mountaineers know that winter is often the best season for mountain walking. There are far fewer people about and it is possible to walk all day without seeing a soul. Most of the routes in this guide were surveyed during the winter and were the source of some truly memorable days. It is impossible to describe to those who have never experienced it the magic of standing on a snow-covered mountain top with the winter sun, low on the horizon, blazing down from an azure sky. On such days it is good to be alive!

Mountain walking in winter is not to be undertaken lightly. I have been on the Sugar Loaf (see route 25) in a white-out when I could not see the trig point until I was 6 ft from it; I have turned back from Craig Cwareli (see routes 11 and 14) because the path has been solid ice and one small slip would have sent me over the precipice; and the strength of the wind has forced me to keep well away from the edge of Craig Fan-las (see route 11) to avoid being blown over.

It is the mark of an experienced mountain walker that he never hesitates to turn back should circumstances warrant; only the foolhardy regard retreat as shameful.

Clothing and equipment required for winter walking includes heavyweight windproof cagoule and overtrousers, boots and gaiters, fibrepile, Thinsulate, Hollofil or down jackets (or many layers of sweaters), a balaclava and windproof gloves, and an ice-axe and crampons. Carry plenty of food and a Thermos flask, a torch and whistle, survival bag, map and compass.

Everyone enjoying the facilities of the National Park should be aware that irresponsible behaviour may put at risk crops and livestock and affect adversely the welcome that those who follow may receive.

Enjoy the countryside and respect its life and work
Guard against all risk of fire
Fasten all gates
Keep your dogs under close control
Keep to public paths across farmland
Use gates and stiles to cross fences, hedges and walls
Leave livestock, crops and machinery alone
Take your litter home
Help to keep all water clean
Protect wildlife, plants and trees
Take care on country roads
Make no unnecessary noise

Remember the motto of American backpackers: Take nothing but photographs; kill nothing but time; leave nothing behind but your footprints and your thanks.

The Landscape of the National Park

Visitors unacquainted with the National Park may be excused if they find some of the place names confusing. The Brecon Beacons are a small group of mountains to the south of Brecon and include the summits of Pen y Fan, Corn Du and Cribyn. This group has given its name to the whole National Park, although the Brecon Beacons themselves occupy only a very small proportion of the total area. Confusion is worse confounded because the western area of the Park is known as the Black Mountain (though it includes many summits) and the eastern area is called the Black Mountains.

The National Park can be divided into five fairly distinct regions. To the west is the Black Mountain, which includes the summits of the Carmarthen Fans and the wild gorge of the Afon Twrch valley. Between the A4067 and the A4059 lies the more undulating country of the Fforest Fawr, which was once a royal hunting forest. South of Fforest Fawr lies the waterfall country, which is quite different in character. This is limestone country, with hills rather than mountains and with numerous cave systems. East of Fforest Fawr are the Brecon Beacons proper, which include the highest mountains in south Wales. Pen y Fan is nearly 3,000 ft high and only 600 ft lower than the top of Snowdon. East of the Usk valley and the A40 are the Black Mountains, which have long valleys extending into them like the fingers of a hand. Above the valleys are long ridges along which it is possible to walk for miles. Indeed, one of the features of all the upland areas of the National Park is the considerable number of long walks which can be taken along the ridges and flat tops of the mountains. It is possible to walk for miles above the 2,000-ft contour line with only occasional short descents.

The Forestry Commission has been active in the National Park and have clothed many of the mountain slopes in the alien green of larch and Sitka spruce, which are not native to the region. From an aesthetic point of view it is a pity that the landscape of such a beautiful region should be changed so dramatically by a form of afforestation which is out of character with the indigenous woodland. There is something so eerie about these silent trees that most forms of wildlife seem to shun them.

Many of the narrow valleys of the National Park have been dammed and reservoirs have been constructed to provide water for south Wales. Although this often results in the loss of good farm land, the effects rarely seem to be as visually unpleasant as the conifer plantations which often screen them.

Most visitors to the National Park come to enjoy the scenery. They must do, for there is little else to attract them. The archaeological remains are few; there are no great churches, cathedrals or castles, and although some of the towns and villages are pleasant enough they cannot compare with the beautiful domestic architecture of Cumbria or the Yorkshire Dales. Apart from walking, the only activities which make this Park popular are pony trekking and caving. It is hoped that this guide will tempt at least some motorists to leave their vehicles in the car park and to enjoy at first hand the glorious scenery of this beautiful National Park.

Geology

The predominant rock in the National Park is Old Red Sandstone, which is composed of marls, flagstones, sandstones, grits and conglomerates. Pressure has tilted the strata and on the southern edge the younger rocks of carboniferous limestone, millstone grit and the coal measures overlie the Old Red Sandstone. The highest mountains have characteristic flat tops caused by a hard layer of conglomerate, which has to some extent protected the softer rock from erosion. The north-facing escarpments have been fashioned by the action of glaciers, which were also responsible for Llangorse Lake.

Archaeology and Antiquities

In mesolithic times the valleys of the National Park were probably the haunt of nomadic hunters who have left no trace of their passing. Later, neolithic farmers established settlements in the Usk valley and started to clear the forests with axe and fire. This process was continued by the ubiquitous Bronze Age Beaker people and their successors, the Celtic tribes who introduced iron. It was these Iron Age settlers who constructed the forts on Table Mountain above Crickhowell (see routes 18 and 20), on Pen-y-crug, north-west of Brecon, and at Carn Gech, above the Towy valley, west of Llandeilo.

When the Romans subdued the area they built forts at Y Gaer, west of Brecon, at Y Pigwyn, just north of the Usk reservoir, and at Coelbren, on the southern boundary of the National Park. The Roman road, Sarn Helen, which can still be traced in parts, crosses the Park from Brecon to Coelbren.

The Normans built motte and bailey castles at Crickhowell, Brecon and Tretower, this last having been restored in recent years. Cerreg Cennen (see route 1) was built in the first half of the thirteenth century and was largely rebuilt some 50 years later. It was partially dismantled in 1462.

At Llanthony (see route 27) are the remains of the Priory founded in the late eleventh century by William de Lacy and incorporated as an Augustinian Priory in 1118. The present church, now a ruin, was built in the early thirteenth century. In 1807 it was bought by Walter Savage Landor, who restored the south tower which today forms part of the Abbey Hotel.

Further up the valley lies Capel-y-ffin, where Father Ignatius (1857–1908) tried to revive Benedictine monasticism in the Church of England. He was a splendid eccentric and a genuinely saintly man, claiming to have received visions of Our Lady in a burning bush. He conducted ceremonies of such lavishness and extravagance that they would have raised the eyebrows of a Renaissance master of ceremonies at the Vatican. In 1924 the monastery was bought by Eric Gill, who worked here for some time. It is now a ruin. David Jones, the poet and artist, joined Gill and recalled his time here in *In Parenthesis*.

Henry Vaughan was born and lived for most of his life at Llansantffraed, Powys, known in his day as Newton on Usk. He practised medicine and wrote much of his poetry at his home here. He is buried outside the east wall of the church.

Glossary of Welsh Place Names

Welsh is the most musical of languages full of subtle rhythms, lilts and cadences. Even the clumsy Saxon tongue can be transformed into something delightful when spoken by a Welshman. The following list of words occur frequently on maps and it is useful to know their meanings.

Aber	the fall of one water into a greater
Afon	river
Allt	wooded hill
Ban, bannau	peak
Bedd	grave
Blaen	head of a valley
Bont	bridge
Bre	hill
Bryn	hill
Bwlch	pass, col
Caer	fort
Capel	chapel
Carn, carnedd	cairn, burial mound
Carreg	stone, rock
Castell	castle
Cefn	ridge
Clwyd	gate
Clyd	cosy
Craig	crag
Crib	ridge
Crug	hillock, mound
Cwm, cymoedd, cymau	valley, cirque
Din, dinas	fortification
Dyffryn, dyffrynnoed	valley
Du, dhu	black
Eglwys, eglwysi, eglwysau, eglwysydd	church
Esgair	escarpment, ridge
Fach	small
Fal	valley
Fan	peak
Fawr	extensive, large

Glossary of Welsh Place Names

Fechan	small
Felindre	mill
Foel	bare hill
Glyder	sheltered valley
Glyn	valley, glen
Gwaun	open moor
Haford	summer residence
Hen	old
Hendre	winter residence
Heol	paved way
Llan	enclosed place, church village
Llyn, llynnoed, llynau	lake
Maen	stone
Mawr	big, great
Moel	bare hill
Mynydd	mountain
Nant, naint, nantydd, nannau	valley, stream
Neuadd	hall
Oge, ogof	cave
Pant	field
Pen	hill
Penmaen	rocky hill
Pistyll	waterfall
Plas	hall, place
Pont, pontydd	bridge
Porth, pyrth	landing place
Pwll	pool
Rhaeadr, rhaiadr	waterfall
Rhiw	hill
Rhos	moor
Sarn	causeway
Sgwd	waterfall
Tir, tiroedd	land
Tre, tref	village, hamlet
Twmp	tump
Twrch	pig
Ty, tai	house
Tyn	small farm
Uch	higher
Uchaf	highest
Uchel	high
Y, yr	the
Ynys	island
Ystrad	valley
Ystwyth	winding

Book List

The area included within the boundaries of the National Park has few literary associations and no significant writer has made it his own. In his celebrated walking tour of Wales undertaken in 1854 and described in *Wild Wales* George Borrow devotes Chapters 47 and 48 to describing his adventures between Llandovery and Brynamon. He relates a hilarious story about the spiritual conversion of the bibulous Vicar of Llandovery from drunkenness to sanctity. Borrow drank a glass of bad beer and argued about religion in Llangadog, and followed what is now the A4069 to Brynamon (which he calls by its old name of Gutter Vawr).

Barber, Christopher, *Exploring the Brecon Beacons National Park: A Walker's Guide to the Brecon Beacons, Waterfall Country and Black Mountains*, Regional Publications, 1980.

Borrow, George, *Wild Wales* (various editions).

Davies, Margaret E., ed., *The Brecon Beacons National Park Guide*, 2nd edn, HMSO, 1978.

Howell, Peter, and Beazley, Elisabeth, *Companion Guide to South Wales*, Collins, 1977.

Kilvert, Rev. Francis, *Diaries*, 3 vols., Cape, 1976 (abridged edn, Penguin Books, 1977.

Poucher, W. A., *The Welsh Peaks: A Pictorial Guide to Walking in This Region and to the Safe Ascent of its Principal Mountain Groups*, 5th edn, Constable, 1973.

Tomes, John, ed., *Blue Guide to Wales*, 6th edn, Ernest Benn, 1979.

Verey, David, *Shell Guide to Mid-Wales*, Faber, 1960.

Ward Lock, *Complete Wales*.

Guide and Route Maps

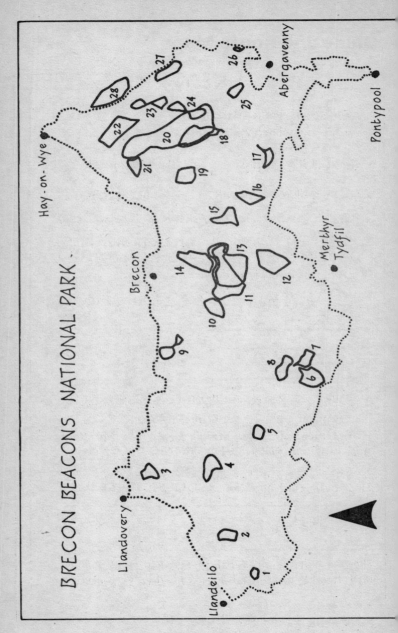

BRECON BEACONS NATIONAL PARK.

KEY

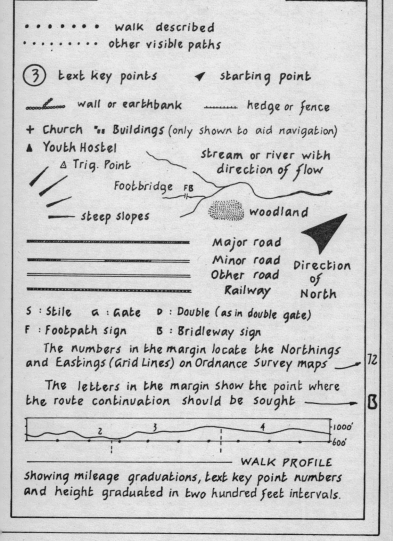

• • • • • • • • walk described

• • • • • • • • • other visible paths

③ text key points ◄ starting point

━━━━━━ wall or earthbank ╌╌╌╌╌ hedge or fence

✝ Church •• Buildings (only shown to aid navigation)

▲ Youth Hostel

△ Trig. Point

stream or river with direction of flow

Footbridge FB

steep slopes woodland

━━━━━━━━ Major road

━━━━━━━━ Minor road

━━━━━━━━ Other road Direction of North

▬▬▬▬▬▬ Railway

S : Stile G : Gate D : Double (as in double gate)

F : Footpath sign B : Bridleway sign

The numbers in the margin locate the Northings and Eastings (Grid Lines) on Ordnance Survey maps ⎯ 72

The letters in the margin show the point where the route continuation should be sought ⟶ B

2 3 4 ‑1000' ‑600'

⎯⎯⎯⎯⎯⎯⎯⎯⎯⎯⎯⎯ WALK PROFILE

showing mileage graduations, text key point numbers and height graduated in two hundred feet intervals.

Route 1. Beddau'r Derwyddon, Hen-grofft, Cerreg Cennen Castle, Cwmcennen, Beddau'r Derwyddon

An easy well-waymarked walk through woods and fields

Distance: 4½ miles
For: Walkers only

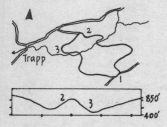

Terrain: Easy
Route-Finding: Easy
Maps: 1:25000 Brecon Beacons Outdoor Leisure Map, Western Area; 1:50000 sheet 159
Start: Beddau'r Derwyddon, 1½ miles south-east of Trapp, grid reference SN674180
Parking: Plentiful at the start of the walk
Buses: None
Refreshments: None

1   Park at the bend in the road and take the grassy track which runs northwards to a waymarked gate and stile. Cross the stile and go straight up the hill across an open field aiming for a solitary tree. Follow the track past the tree, make for the wire fence ahead and continue to a waymarked stile in the far left-hand corner of the field. *Do not cross this stile* but make for the gate at the far end of the field. Pass through the gate and follow the clear track which hugs the left-hand headland. Go downhill, taking the left-hand fork, to a sharp hairpin bend and a gate on the clearly defined farm track to Hen-grofft. Pass through the gates of the farmyard and cross the bridge at the river. Immediately turn right and pass through a gate to walk up the left-hand side of the stream, passing two waymarked stiles on the way. Follow the river until you see the waymark directing you round a hairpin bend and up into the wood. Follow the broad grassy path out of the wood and up the hill to where it curves round the left-hand side of the castle (*see p. 23*).

2   Follow the obvious route towards the car park but turn left just before the bridge and walk down the side of a barn to a gate in a wire fence. Pass through this gate and continue forward to another gate which gives access to a metalled lane. Turn left and follow the lane for 100 yds to where it bends sharply left. Pass through the gate on the right set in a massive stone pillar and walk down the left-hand headland to a gap in the hedge at the bottom of the field. Pass through the gap and continue forward to another gap which gives access to an enclosed lane.

3   Follow the lane to a gate and a stile. The track then bears left towards a farm and passes through a gate into the farmyard. Almost immediately, turn left and go down the side of a barn to a track which crosses the path. Bear right and follow this sunken track to a gate and on to a gap. At the gap, the track enters an open field and becomes less distinct. Continue forward across the field to a wood where the track becomes visible again. Just

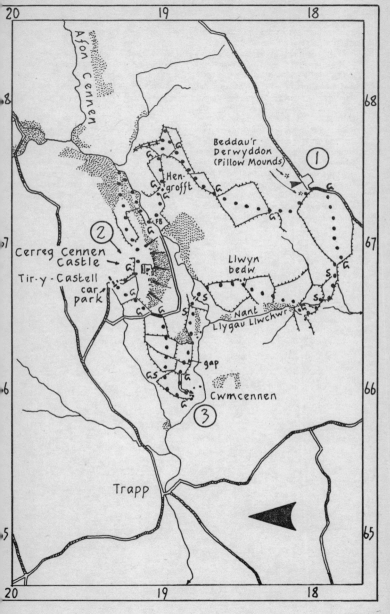

Afon Cennen

Beddau'r
Derwyddon
(Pillow Mounds)

①

Hen-
grofft

FB

②

Cerreg Cennen
Castle

Tir-y-Castell
car
park

Llwyn
bedw

Nant
Llygau Llwchwr

gap

Cwmcennen

③

Trapp

inside the wood the track forks. Take the left-hand fork and walk uphill to reach a gap which leads into an open field. Turn left and follow the headland to the top of the field. Turn right and follow the headland to another gap and make for the stile now visible on the right-hand side at the bottom of the field. Cross the waymarked stile and walk to the river. In normal conditions the river can be forded. Towards the top of the field a stile is visible; cross it and follow the waymarked direction using the left-hand headland. At the top of the field turn right and walk the length of the house to the farm track. Follow the track across a cattle grid to reach a ford and another cattle grid. Continue along the broad metalled track for a few yards until it crosses a stream and take the next waymarked gate on the left. Follow a broad track to a gate and waymarked stile giving access to a wet sunken lane which follows the left-hand bank of a stream to a waymarked gate and stile. Cross the stile and bear right, following the track and noting the ruined tower on the left. After the fenced-off source of the stream, the track is less distinct and becomes a broad grassy path. Follow it round, keeping the hedge on your right, to reach a gate in a wire fence. Keep the tumuli on your right and you will come to a waymarked stile which gives access to a road. Turn left and follow the road to your car.

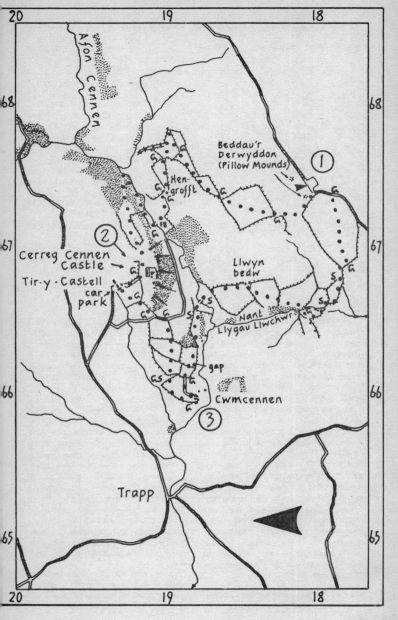

20   19   18

Afon Cennen

68

Beddau'r
Derwyddon
(Pillow Mounds)

①

Hen-
grofft

G

68

67

②

Cerreg Cennen
Castle →

Tir-y-Castell
car
park

Llwyn
bedw

67

Nant
Llygau Llwchwr

gap

Cwmcennen

66

③

66

Trapp

65

65

20   19   18

Route 2. From Capel Gwynfe

An easy walk through lanes and fields

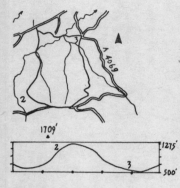

Distance: 5 miles
For: Walkers only
Terrain: Easy
Route-finding: Easy
Maps: 1:25000 Brecon Beacons Outdoor Leisure Map, Western Area; 1:50000 sheet 160
Start: The school at Capel Gwynfe, grid reference S N716215
Parking: Roadside parking at the start of the walk
Buses: None
Refreshments: None

1 Take the metalled path that runs along the left-hand side of the school and continue to a gate. Walk downhill to a gate at the bottom right-hand corner of the field. Continue forward to a gate ahead and walk down the right-hand headland to a gate at the end. On reaching the gate that gives access to a roughly metalled track, turn right along the track and pass through the gates on either side of the farmyard, to reach an enclosed track. Walk down to the ford, cross the stream by the footbridge and walk up to the farm gate ahead. In the middle of the farmyard turn left and pass through a gate to follow a tributary stream on the left, keeping some modern farm buildings on the right. The very muddy track follows the stream until reaching a ruined farm. Pass through a gate giving access to the farm, and walk up the left-hand side of the farmhouse into an open field.

2 Walk up the left-hand headland of the field and pass through a gate to enter an enclosed lane. After a few yards the enclosed lane peters out into a field. Turn left and walk up the left-hand headland to a gate, then up the right-hand headland of the next field. Pass through a gap and cross an enclosed track which runs left down to a ruined farm. Continue forward and walk across the field to a gap, keeping the pine trees on your left. Pass through the gap and continue to a gate on the left at the top of the field. Pass through this gate and follow the clear track, which runs parallel to a fence on the left to reach a road. Continue along the road for a short distance until it bears slightly right and begins to climb. At this point bear left along a grassy track which descends to a farm. Pass through the farmyard and walk down the farm road to the main road.

3 Turn left and almost immediately left again to walk down a minor road for a few yards before turning left again into

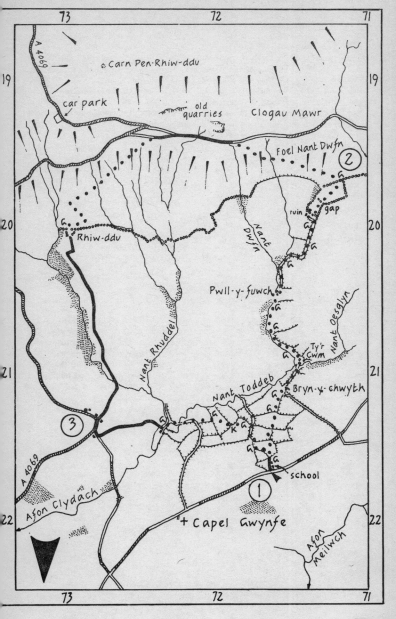

A 4069

Carn Pen·Rhiw·ddu

car park

old quarries

Clogau Mawr

Foel Nant Dwfn

②

Nant Dwfn

ruin

gap

Rhiw·ddu

Pwll·y·fuwch

Nant Oesglyn

Ty'r Cwm

Nant Rhuddel

Nant Toddeb

Bryn·y·chwyth

③

A 4069

Afon Clydach

school

①

✝ Capel Gwynfe

Afon Meilwch

a metalled lane. At a farm it bears left to reach a gate. Pass through the gate and turn right down a rough enclosed lane to a footbridge. Cross it and walk up the right-hand headland of the field. At the top of the field, turn left and follow the headland to a gate on the right. Pass through the gate and then cross diagonally over the field to a kissing gate and on to a gap and a ford. Continue forward to the gate ahead, and turn right on to a metalled farm lane. Almost immediately turn right again to walk up an enclosed muddy lane. At the top, bear left to continue along the enclosed lane, and pass through a gate into a field. Follow the path diagonally up the field to a line of gorse bushes which brings you to reach the gate near the school and your car.

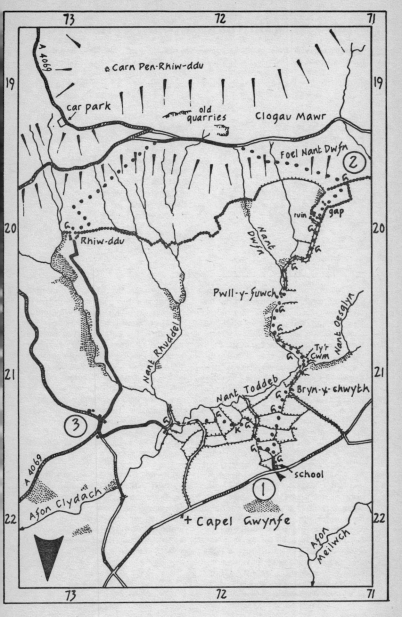

73   72   71

A 4069

⚹ Carn Pen-Rhiw-ddu

19

car park   old quarries   Clogau Mawr

Foel Nant Dwfn

②

ruin   gap

20

Rhiw-ddu

Nant Dwfn

Pwll-y-fuwch

Nant Oesglyn

Nant Rhuddel

Ty'r Cwm

21   Nant Toddeb   Bryn-y-chwyth   21

③

A 4069

school

①

Afon Clydach

22   ✝ Capel Gwynfe   22

Afon Meilwch

73   72   71

Route 3. Myddfai and the Usk Reservoir

A fairly easy walk which includes some open moorland and has fine views over the Usk Reservoir

Distance: 5½ miles
For: Walkers and riders
Terrain: Moderately difficult
Route-finding: Easy

Maps: 1:25000 Brecon Beacons Outdoor Leisure Map, Western Area; 1:50000 sheet 160
Start: Cwm-Clyd, 1 mile east of Myddfai, grid reference S N790303
Parking: Limited roadside parking at the start of the walk
Buses: None
Refreshments: None

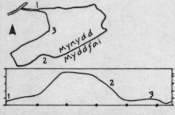

1 Park near Cwm-clyd Farm, then follow the road, which deteriorates at the far end, to a gate on the moorland edge. Pass through the gate and follow the clearly defined path up the hill. (Note that the official line of the path roughly follows the line of the telegraph poles, but ignore these as the track is a much easier route.) On descending the hill, the track reaches a junction of paths at some mounds which are the remains of old mine workings. Turn left, walk towards the hill and after 50 yds or so turn right and follow a clearly defined grassy path which runs above the mine workings parallel to the forest. Take the path which forks off to the right just after passing through a very boggy patch and a dip. This seems to peter out after a bit, but continue making for the highest ground until reaching the trig point. Continue on beyond the trig point for about a mile, when the path bears off to the right and soon becomes less distinct. Follow it, making sure not to drop *steeply* downhill, and you will arrive at a stone wall with a gate in it.

2 Pass through the gate, go downhill through another gate in a wire fence, and then, reaching another wire fence, turn right along a track. Follow the track downhill until almost reaching a road and a house. About 30 yds before reaching the road, turn right through the second of two adjacent gates and follow the fence and hedge on your right. Pass through a gate at the far end of the field and continue forward, keeping the fence on your left. Continue following the wire fence for ¼ mile until reaching a broad, stony track which bears off to the right up the mountain side.

3 Ignore this track and turn left through the next gate on the left and aim for the farm ahead. Cross the ford at a gate and keep down the left-hand headland, passing through a gate at either end of the farmyard. Follow the farm drive to the road, turn right and walk to your car.

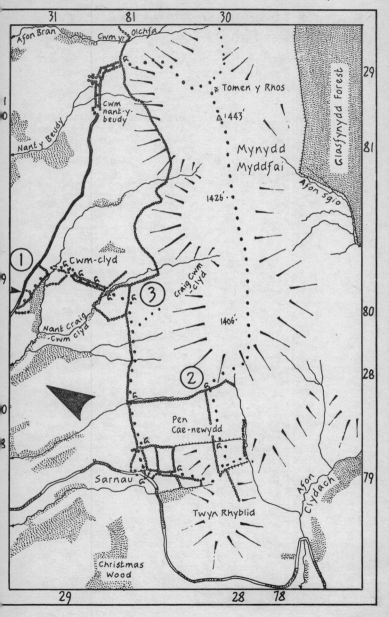

Route 4. Llanddeusant and the Carmarthen Fans

A splendid walk across open country climbing to 2,500 ft. There are magnificent views

Distance: 9 miles
For: Walkers and riders
Terrain: Difficult

Route-finding: Moderately difficult
Maps: 1:25000 Brecon Beacons Outdoor Leisure Map, Western Area; 1:50000 sheet 160
Start: Llanddeusant, grid reference S N776245
Parking: There is nowhere to park in the narrow lanes around Llanddeusant and it is advisable for walkers to arrange for a car to deliver and collect them. There is a Forestry Commission car park near the Usk Reservoir, grid reference S N820272
Buses: None
Refreshments: None

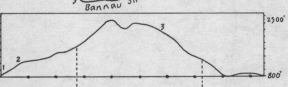

1 Take the road which runs eastwards from the T-junction signposted Llyn y Fan fach and, after a couple of hundred yards or so, bear left and leave the road passing through a gate to enter an enclosed track. At a crossing of enclosed tracks, continue forward, pass through a gate and almost immediately turn right into another enclosed track. Pass through another gate and then the gate at the top leading on to open country.

2 The path can be seen going ahead bearing round the right-hand flank of the hill. Follow the clearly defined path until it drops down towards a stream where it forks. Take the right-hand fork which crosses the stream, and follow the path until it reaches another stream. At this point leave the path and aim for the highest mountain on the left.

Continued on p. 44

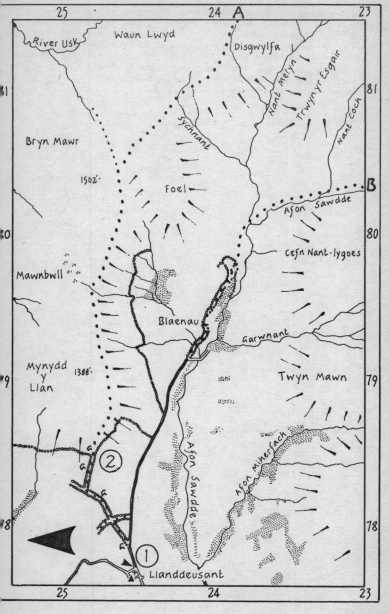

River Usk

Waun Lwyd

25   24   A   23

Disgwylfa

Nant melyn

Trwyn yr Esgair

Nant coch

81   81

Bryn Mawr

Sychnant

1502·

Foel

B

Afon   Sawdde

80   80

Cefn Nant-lygoes

Mawnbwll

Blaenau

Garwnant

Twyn Mawn

Mynydd
y
Llan   1388·

79   79

②

Afon Sawdde

Afon miherfach

78   78

①

Llanddeusant

25   24   23

43

3   Bear left and make for the ridge on the left-hand side of the mountain which provides the easiest access to the summit. At the summit turn right and drop down very steeply, and then climb to another summit. From here the route is fairly level until reaching a cairn, at which point the edge turns round to the right above a lake. Go down the ridge and the path appears to go straight ahead, but bear right and go down more steeply to arrive at the extreme edge of the lake. Follow the roughly metalled track all the way back to Llanddeusant.

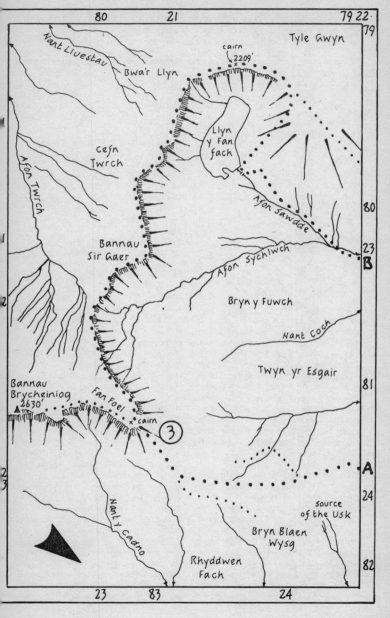

Nant Lluestau

Bwa'r Llyn

Tyle Gwyn

cairn
×2209'

Cefn
Twrch

Llyn
y Fan
fach

Afon Twrch

Afon Sawdde

Bannau
Sir Gaer

Afon Sychlwch

Bryn y Fuwch

Nant Coch

Twyn yr Esgair

Bannau
Brycheiniog
▲2630'

Fan Foel

×cairn

③

A

source
of the Usk

Nant y Cadno

Bryn Blaen
Wysg

Rhyddwen
Fach

Route 5. From Craig-y-Nos Country Park

An easy route mostly through fields but climbing to 1,500 ft on the edge of open country

Distance: 4 miles
For: Walkers only

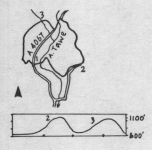

Terrain: Easy
Route-finding: Easy
Maps: 1:25000 Brecon Beacons Outdoor Leisure Map, Western Area; 1:50000 sheet 160
Start: Craig-y-Nos Country Park on the A4067 10½ miles south-west of Sennybridge, grid reference S N840156
Parking: Plentiful at the start of the walk
Buses: South Wales Transport Company Service 117/118 Brecon–Swansea
Refreshments: There is a café in the Country Park

1 Walk to the bottom of the car park, cross the bridge and immediately turn left. Follow the stream along a clear path until reaching a stile and a gate. Cross the stile and turn right to follow a clear path which bears right and then follows the boundary of the Country Park to a metalled lane at a farm. Follow the lane and at the bottom of the hill, just before a gate across the road, turn left through a gate and follow the path uphill to a gate which gives access to the road.

2 Turn left and walk up the road for 200 yds to a bungalow (Hillcrest). Pass through a gate on the left just beyond the bungalow garage and follow the clearly defined path which moves slightly away from the fence and soon drops steeply downhill through some trees to a gate and a stile. Cross the stile and walk down to the farm. Pass through the gates in the farmyard, then follow the metalled lane down to the main road. At the main road turn

left, cross the bridge and walk along the verge, with the inn on the left. Just before the second bridge, turn right through a gate leading to a farm. Follow the stony track past the farm, curve to the left round the outside of the farm and then continue uphill.

3 At the top of the field is a stone wall. The track veers sharply left to a gate giving access to a very rocky and wide stream. Cross the stream by the rocks, turn left and go up the high bank along a narrow, clear path. At the top of the bank the path turns sharp right and becomes much broader and grassier. Follow the broad grassy path which climbs up to the mountain top, following the stone wall on the left. Near the top the path drops down suddenly to an old quarry. Go down into the quarry and up the other side, still following the stone wall. At the first wall that *crosses* the path there is a sheep pen with a very deep quarry on the right-hand side. Keep between

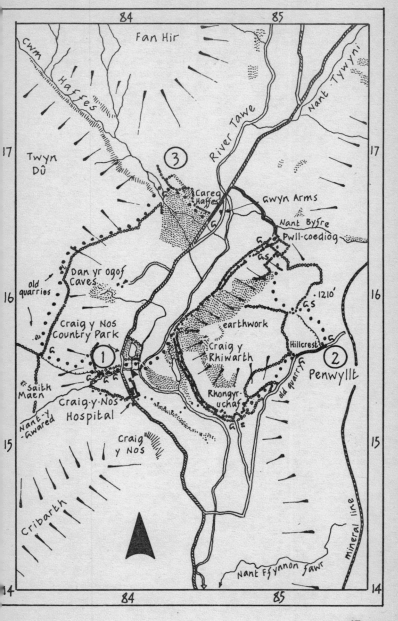

the sheep pen and the wall on your left and you will find a gate on your left. Pass through it and walk downhill, moving slightly away from the fence on your right. After a short way follow a clearly defined sunken path down the hillside to a wall, where it makes a right hairpin bend. Continue to a track at a T-junction near a stream. Turn left and pass through the gate and walk down to the farm, where there are two gates at either end of the farmyard. Pass through them, walking through the farmyard to the road. Turn left and walk the short distance to the main road. Opposite is the Country Park where the walk began.

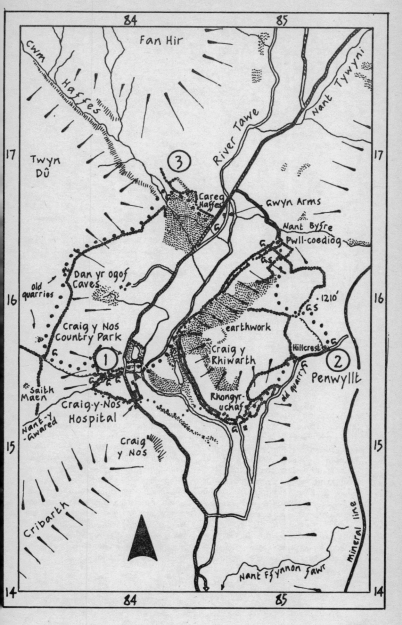

Cwm
Haffes
Fan Hir

84   85

River Tawe   Nant Tywyni

17   17
Twyn
Dû
                    ③
                              Careg
                              Haffes
                                        Gwyn Arms
                                        Nant Byfre
                                        Pwll-coediog

old
quarries   Dan yr ogof
                  Caves
16   · 1210'   16
                              earthwork
          Craig y Nos
          Country Park   Craig y
                                      Rhiwarth   Hillcrest
          ①   ②
    saith   old quarry   Penwyllt
    Maen
          Craig-y-Nos   Rhongyr-
          Hospital   uchaf

Nant-y-
Gwared
15   Craig   15
                  y Nos

Cribarth

                                                    mineral line

14   14
          84   85

                    Nant Ffynnon fawr

Route 6. Pont-Nedd Fechan and the waterfalls of Afon Mellte and Afon Nedd

An easy route following mountain streams with many spectacular waterfalls. At Sgwd yr Eira the river is crossed by walking through the hollow behind the waterfall

Distance: 8½ miles
For: Walkers only

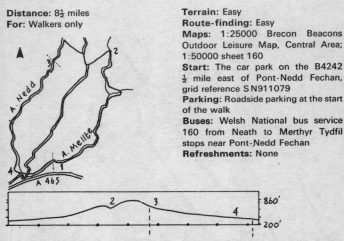

Terrain: Easy
Route-finding: Easy
Maps: 1:25000 Brecon Beacons Outdoor Leisure Map, Central Area; 1:50000 sheet 160
Start: The car park on the B4242 ½ mile east of Pont-Nedd Fechan, grid reference S N911079
Parking: Roadside parking at the start of the walk
Buses: Welsh National bus service 160 from Neath to Merthyr Tydfil stops near Pont-Nedd Fechan
Refreshments: None

1   From the parking place near the Mellte follow the right-hand bank of the stream for just over a mile until reaching a difficult stretch and turn right and follow the Hepste to Sgwd yr Eira waterfall. The path crosses the river behind the waterfall. It may be necessary to put on waterproofs to keep dry. The path is slippery so take care and do not hurry. Follow the obvious path which climbs above the river for about ¼ mile until dropping down to the Mellte again. Continue walking upstream until reaching a footbridge.

2   Cross the Mellte by the bridge, turn left and walk downstream to Sgwd Clun-gwyn falls. Now turn right and

walk up the hillside following a clear track to the road. Turn right, pass a gorge and look for a small chapel on the right. Cross the stile opposite the chapel and walk diagonally across the field, aiming to the right of the farm to reach a gate. Turn right and walk down the enclosed track for a short distance until meeting a metalled farm lane. Turn right and walk along it until it makes a sharp right-hand bend. At this point, go through a gate and walk down the left-hand side down a field to a clump of trees, where there is a ford and a stile beyond. Continue forward over the clearly defined path to another stile in a wire fence and on to the river (Afon Nedd).

Continued on p. 52

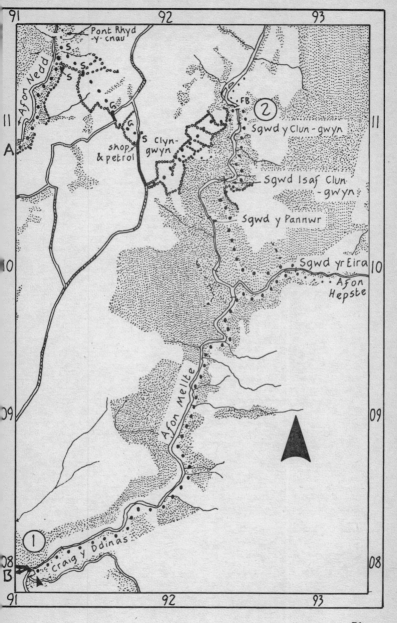

Pont Rhyd
-y-cnau

Afon Nedd

S
S   S
S

G
G

shop
& petrol

S Clyn-
gwyn

FB

② Sgwd y Clun-gwyn

Sgwd Isaf Clun-
-gwyn

Sgwd y Pannwr

Sgwd yr Eira
Afon Hepste

Afon Mellte

①

Craig y Ddinas

A

B

91   92   93

11   11

10   10

09   09

08   08

51

3 Turn left and follow the path down-stream until reaching the road. Turn right, and then immediately left through the picnic area at Pont Melin-fach. Follow the clear riverside walk on the right-hand bank of the river for nearly 2 miles all the way to Pont-Nedd Fechan. On reaching the road, turn left and walk to the parking place.

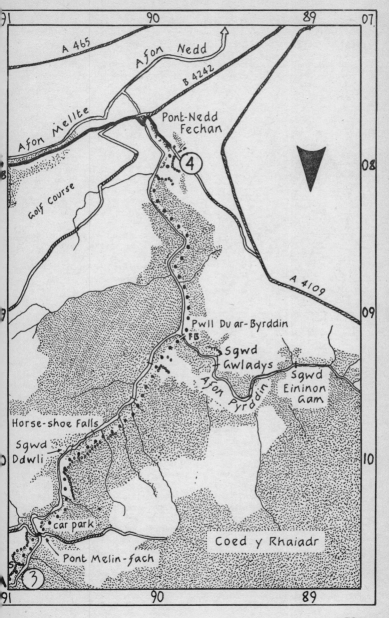

71
90
89
07

A 465

Afon Nedd

B 4242

Afon Mellte

Pont-Nedd
Fechan

④

08

Golf Course

A 4109

09

Pwll Du ar-Byrddin

FB

Sgwd
Gwladys

Afon Pyrddin

Sgwd
Eininon
Gam

Horse-shoe falls

Sgwd
Ddwli

10

car park

Coed y Rhaiadr

Pont Melin-fach

③

91
90
89

Route 7. Penderyn and the waterfalls of Afon Mellte and Afon Hepste

A lowland route visiting some spectacular waterfalls including Sgwd yr Eira, where the river is crossed by walking through the hollow behind the waterfall

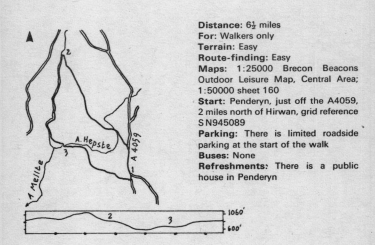

Distance: 6½ miles
For: Walkers only
Terrain: Easy
Route-finding: Easy
Maps: 1:25000 Brecon Beacons Outdoor Leisure Map, Central Area; 1:50000 sheet 160
Start: Penderyn, just off the A4059, 2 miles north of Hirwan, grid reference S N945089
Parking: There is limited roadside parking at the start of the walk
Buses: None
Refreshments: There is a public house in Penderyn

1   Walk along the A4059 towards Brecon. Just before reaching a cattle grid turn left down the track which leads to Caerhowell Farm. Turn off the track through the first gate on the right and walk parallel to the main road until reaching a stile in a wire fence. Cross the stile and continue forward making for the farm on the slope of the hill ahead. Cross a stone stile in a wall and continue forward to make for the bridge in front of the farm. Follow the stony track up towards the farm, turn left in front of the farm, and walk along the side of the farm past an old iron barn. Continue forward up the hill and then follow the track through a gap in a stone wall and round to the right. On reaching rough pasture, pass through a gap in the stone wall, bear slightly right, and make a bee-line for the forest edge at the far end of the

wire fence on the right. At the top of the field cross the stile in the wire fence and a forestry road and continue forward into the forest. On reaching a Forestry Commission track which crosses, continue forward down a much narrower path heading for the farms on the other side of the valley. (The Ordnance Survey shows this section to be forested but it has now been cleared.) Continue forward along an indistinct path to reach the forest edge and a stone wall and a sign which says 'Path Legally Diverted'. Turn left and follow the forest edge. The path drops steeply downhill to a stile and a wire fence. Turn right and follow a track almost to the farm, then bear slightly left and pass through a gate and cross a stile, to reach the road opposite the Cwm-porth picnic area.

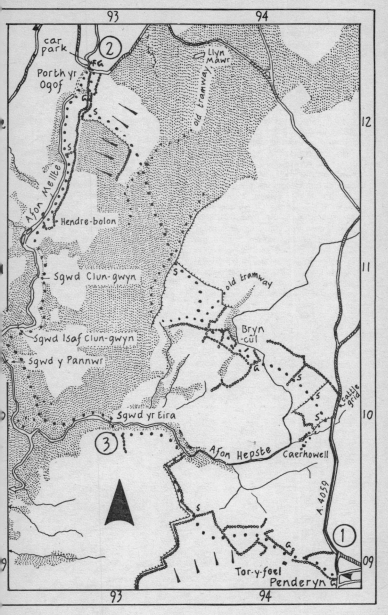

car park

② FG

Porth yr Ogof

Llyn Mawr

old tramway

Afon Mellte

Hendre-bolon

Sgwd Clun-gwyn

old tramway

Sgwd Isaf Clun-gwyn

Bryn -cul

Sgwd y Pannwr

G

S

S

cattle grid

Sgwd yr Eira

③

Afon Hepste

Caerhowell

A.4059

①

S

G

Tor-y-foel

Penderyn

2 Turn left and at the footpath sign opposite the car park, pass through a gate and follow the clearly defined and well-worn path downhill. At this point the stream is underground and cannot be seen. After a couple of hundred yards or so it reappears on the right-hand side of the path. Cross a stile just beyond a picnic area. The path is now much easier to follow. Cross another stile in a wire fence and continue downstream to a footbridge. *Do not cross the footbridge* but continue forward on the left-hand bank of the river. After ½ mile the path climbs steeply up to a grassy col overlooking two valleys. At this point keep to the left and leave the Afon Mellte and enter the Hepste Valley. Very soon the path drops steeply downhill, to the stream. Ignore the path that runs off to the right in a series of steep hairpins down to the river but keep to the higher path which will bring you to the river bank above a series of waterfalls. At a bend in the stream is the magnificent waterfall of Sgwd yr Eira.

On reaching the waterfall, walk behind **3** the flow of water in an area that has been hollowed out by erosion. (It may be necessary to put on waterproofs to keep dry.) Walk through carefully — do not run as it is slippery and one false move could send the unwary over the edge. On the other side, climb up a very steep stony path and walk upstream above the river. On reaching a stile in a wire fence immediately in front of a stone wall, turn right and walk between the fence and the wall. (The path is recorded wrongly on the Ordnance Survey Map.) On reaching a turf and stone wall, turn right over a rudimentary stile, cross a stream and head for the disused quarry ahead, bearing right to follow higher ground to avoid a boggy patch in the hollow. In the quarry is an old tramway track which should be followed to a gate in the farm track which leads to the road following a line of telegraph poles. Pass through a gate at the road and walk to your parking place.

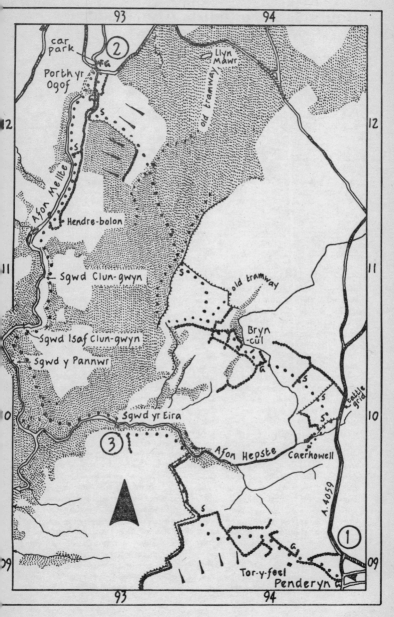

car park

② FG

Porth yr
Ogof

Llyn
Mawr

old tramway

Afon Mellte

Hendre-bolon

S

S

Sgwd Clun-gwyn

S

old tramway

Bryn
-cŵl

Sgwd Isaf Clun-gwyn

Sgwd y Pannwr

G

S

S

Sgwd yr Eira

S

Cattle
grid

③

Afon Hepste

Caerhowell

A.4059

S

G

Tor-y-foel

①

09

09

Penderyn

93

94

12

12

11

11

10

10

57

Route 8. Ystradfellte, Afon Nedd, Porth yr Ogof, Ystradfellte

A lowland circuit linking two valleys

Distance: 5½ miles
For: Walkers only

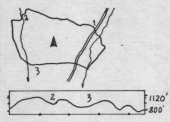

Terrain: Easy
Route-finding: Moderately difficult
Maps: 1:25000 Brecon Beacons Outdoor Leisure Map, Central Area; 1:50000 sheet 160
Start: The car park in Ystradfellte, 6 miles north of Hirwan, grid reference SN930135
Parking: Plentiful at the start of the walk
Buses: None
Refreshments: There is a public house in Ystradfellte

1 On leaving the car park in Ystradfellte, turn left and follow a metalled lane. Where the tarmac ends is a crossing of tracks. Continue forward and pass through a series of gates to emerge at the top into open country. At this point the wall forms a right angle. Take an angle of 45° midway between the two walls and aim for a clump of trees on the hillside from where it may be possible to see an indistinct path that runs forward to a stone wall well to the right of a small wood. Aim for a gate in this wall and make for it climbing a steep bank. At the top is a field and although the path is indistinct it is clearly visible right at the end, near the wall, where it goes through the bracken. Make for the path and pass through the broken wall, climb the bank to the top, where there is a gully with an indistinct grassy path going down bearing slightly to the right. Follow this and it soon becomes much clearer going through a broken turf wall and bearing right to reach a wire fence. Follow the fence to the end and turn left to reach the road. Turn left, pass through the gate and walk along

the road until reaching a tarmac lane going off to the right. Follow the lane until it ends at a gated bridge.

Cross the bridge and follow the broad **2** track until reaching the edge of the conifer forest. Pass through a stone wall and take the track which runs off to the left. After a few hundred yards, pass a ruined building on the right. At this point leave the track which bears right to follow the forest edge. Fork left and walk down the hill keeping the stone wall on the left to reach a ruined building and a stile. Cross the stile and turn right to follow the headland until reaching the fenced bank of the river passing through a gap in a stone wall on the way. Continue along the stream passing through several gaps in field boundaries, always keeping the wire fence on the left. At the end of enclosed country there is a stile in a wire fence. Cross the field making for the bottom left-hand corner where the path becomes more distinct as it enters a wood. Cross some awkward rocky slabs and continue over rough pasture to a ruined building. The path

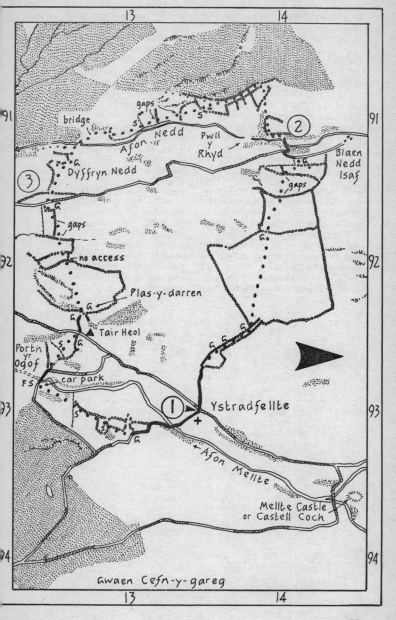

13 14

91 91

bridge gaps

s

Afon Nedd

Pwll y Rhyd

②

Blaen Nedd Isaf

Dyffryn Nedd

③

gaps

gaps

92 92

no access

Plas-y-darren

Tair Heol

Porth yr Ogof

s

FS

car park

s

①

Ystradfellte

+

Afon Mellte

93 93

Mellte Castle or Castell Coch

94 94

Gwaen Cefn-y-gareg

13 14

goes to the right of the building and then immediately turns left and drops down to the stream. Cross the bridge and follow a wet and stony track to the barn at the top of the hill. Pass through the gate on the left-hand side of the barn to reach a farm track which runs to the road.

3   Cross the road and enter the gate opposite. The path moves slightly away from a wire fence on the right and passes through a series of peat or turf banks. You will see a bit of stone wall below you with a gap. Make for the gap in the wall below and then walk up the hill side towards another gap in a stone wall. Continue forward making for the far left-hand corner of the field. There should be access through the wall at this point but it may be necessary to turn right at the wall and walk along it until finding a suitable crossing point, retracing the route on the other side of the wall. Climb to the top of the hill where there are two quarries. Pass between them (there is no path at first but it suddenly becomes visible near a small water hole) and drop down the hillside following the path to come out at the back of a farm. Turn right at a gate into the farmyard and out through a gate on the other side on to a metalled lane. Walk down the lane to the road. Pass through the gate opposite and walk down the left-hand headland to a stile. Cross the stile and continue down the left-hand headland to another stile. Cross it and continue down the left-hand headland to a stile and footpath sign at the road. Turn right and walk along the road to Cwm-porth car park. Walk towards the toilets and cross the stile in the fence beside them. *Do not descend towards the river* but continue forward to reach a field. *Do not enter the field* but bear right. Cross a stone wall and follow the path through the wood to a gate at the road. Turn left and walk into Ystradfellte.

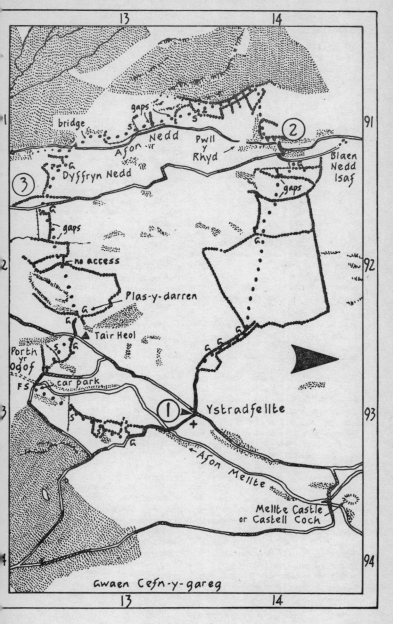

Route 9. From the Brecon Beacons Mountain Centre

A lowland route along tracks and across fields

Distance: 8 miles
For: Walkers only (this route is entirely along bridleways but at the time of the survey some gates would not open)

Terrain: Easy
Route-finding: Easy
Maps: 1:25000 Brecon Beacons Outdoor Leisure Map, Central Area; 1:50000 sheet 160
Start: The Brecon Beacons Mountain Centre 5½ miles west of Brecon, grid reference S N977263
Parking: Plentiful at the start of the walk
Buses: National Welsh Omnibus Service 170 from Aberdare to Brecon stops at Libanus, 1 mile from the start of the walk
Refreshments: Available at the Mountain Centre

1. From the car park take the road leading to Llanilltyd hamlet. Pass the church on your left and continue on the road to the cattle grid, at which turn left and follow the stone wall along a grassy track. Where the wall swings to the left, go forward until reaching the road. At the road take the grassy enclosed path opposite. Follow it for nearly ¾ mile, passing through several gates, some of which will not open and have to be climbed. Suddenly the path drops downhill and ends abruptly against a wire fence, the boundary of a wood.

2. Turn left here and follow the field edge to the bottom of the field where there is a gate topped with barbed wire. Cross this and you will be in an enclosed track. Turn left and walk down the hill. At the bottom of the field turn right and walk to the end of the field to a gate above a stream. Pass through the gate into a sunken track which follows the stream, passes through a gate and then reaches a footbridge and ford at the confluence of streams. Cross the stream, turn right and follow the track to the farm. Take the gate on the left and pass through the farmyard to the road. Turn left and continue straight ahead. After passing the first turn-off to the left, walk up the hill and take the right-hand fork. About 250 yds on the left is a gate giving access to a grassy enclosed path. The gate is obstructed with wire, but can be climbed. Pass through the gate and climb the hill through several gates until reaching the open moor. Pass through the last gate and

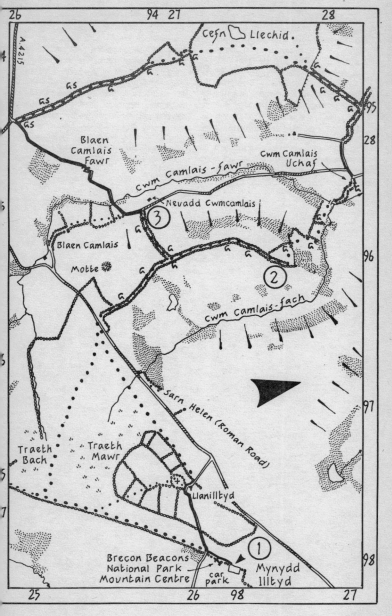

26   94   27   28

Cefn ⌂ Llechid.

A.4215

GS
GS
GS
GS

Blaen
Camlais
Fawr

Cwm Camlais
Uchaf

Cwm Camlais - Fawr

Nevadd Cwmcamlais

③

Blaen Camlais

Motte ✳

②

Cwm Camlais - Fach

Sarn Helen (Roman Road)

Traeth
Bach

Traeth
Mawr

Llanilltyd

①

Brecon Beacons
National Park
Mountain Centre

car
park

Mynydd
Illtyd

25   26   98   27

28

95

28

96

97

98

63

continue for 30 yds to a junction of three tracks. Take the centre one (the broadest) and continue along it, ignoring paths that cross. A trig point is on the right and the path passes close to three ponds and to the left of a tumulus-like hillock. Continue on until reaching a gate in a stone wall. Pass through it and follow the sunken track along a stone wall. Continue through a series of gates until reaching the main road. Here, turn sharp left along the *minor* road and follow it to where it drops down to cross a stream and then turns sharp left.

200 yds after crossing the stream, and just before reaching Neuadd Cwm-camlais, turn right along a stony track. Walk up the track to a gate at the top and the grassy path near the beginning of the walk. Turn right, walk to the road, cross over it and take the broad grassy path which bears slightly leftwards. In places there seem to be several paths, but generally speaking walk in a straight line, though if in doubt bear slightly left. On reaching a wall turn left along a broad grassy track which will return you to the start.

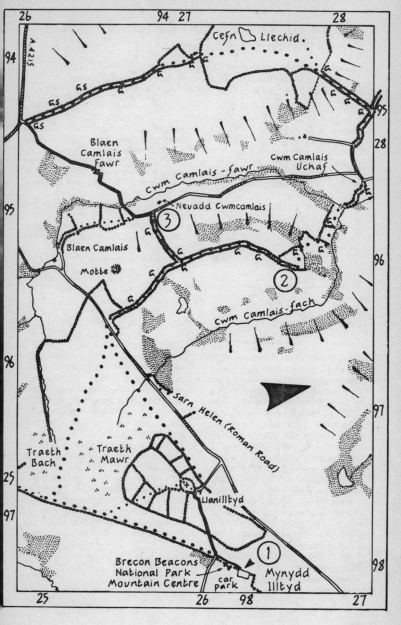

A 4215

94

95

95

96

96

97

25

97

Cefn Llechid.

Gs
Gs
Gs

Blaen
Camlais
Fawr

Cwm Camlais - fawr

Cwm Camlais
Uchaf

Nevadd Cwmcamlais

③

G

Blaen Camlais

Motte

G

G

G

②

Cwm Camlais - fach

Sarn Helen (Roman Road)

Traeth
Bach

Traeth
Mawr

Llanilltyd

①

Brecon Beacons
National Park
Mountain Centre

car
park

Mynydd
Illtyd

26   94   27   28

28

95

96

97

98

25   26   98   27

Route 10. The Brecon Beacons from the Storey Arms

The shortest and easiest route to the top of Corn Du at 2,863 feet, the second highest point in the Brecon Beacons. In fine weather this route can be attempted by novice walkers, providing that they are fit

Distance: 5½ miles
For: Walkers only
Terrain: Moderately difficult
Route-finding: Easy

Maps: 1:25000 Brecon Beacons Outdoor Leisure Map, Central Area; 1:50000 sheet 160
Start: The Storey Arms Youth Adventure Centre on the A470 12 miles south-west of Brecon, grid reference SN983204
Parking: Plentiful at the start of the walk
Buses: National Welsh Omnibus Service 170 Aberdare- Brecon stops at the Storey Arms
Refreshments: None

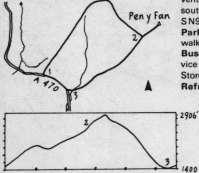

1 Cross the stile near the telephone box and follow the clear path up the mountain side, moving slightly away from the wire fence on the right. Keep to the high ground as there are several paths which run off to the right and drop down to the stream on the right. Cross a ladder stile, pass the source of the stream and then make your way along a clear path towards the very steep ridge which leads up to Corn Du. The path passes the obelisk which 'marks the spot where the body of Tommy Jones aged 5 was found. He lost his way between Cwmllwch Farm and the Login on the night of August 4th 1900. After an anxious search of 29 days his remains were discovered Sept. 2nd. Erected by voluntary subscriptions. W. Powell Price Mayor of Brecon 1900.' This is a very steep climb indeed

2 On reaching the top those who want to extend their walk should turn left and walk along the edge, admiring the magnificent view. They can then retrace their steps. Those who now wish to return to their car should turn right, keeping the edge on their right, and after a short distance they will descend very steeply (in windy weather this can be extremely dangerous) for a short distance to pick up the main path which bears off to the right down towards the reservoir. Near an obelisk, cross the stream by some stepping stones, climb some steps and go through a kissing gate to reach the road. Turn right and walk back to your car.

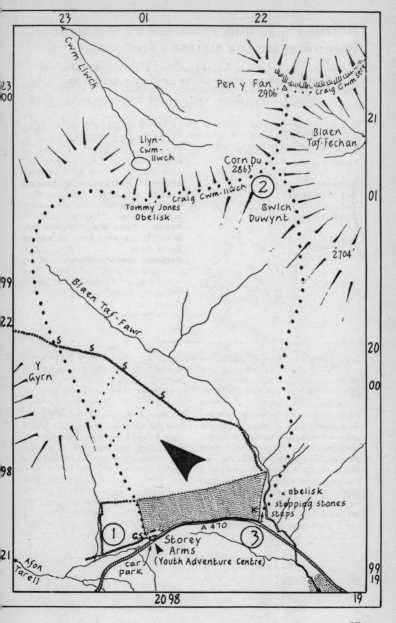

23 01 22

Cwm Llwch

Pen y Fan
2906'

Craig Cwm sere

23
00

Blaen
Taf·Fechan

21

Llyn-
Cwm-
llwch

Corn Du
2863'

Craig Cwm-llwch

2

01

Tommy Jones
Obelisk

Bwlch
Duwynt

99

Blaen Taf·Fawr

2704'

22

5 5

5

20

Y
Gyrn

5

00

98

obelisk
stepping stones
steps

K

1

GS

A 470

3

Storey
Arms
(Youth Adventure Centre)

99
19

21

Afon
Tarell

car
Park

2098

19

67

Route 11. Grand Traverse of the Brecon Beacons: Upper Neuadd Reservoir, Craig Fan-ddu, Corn Du, Pen y Fan, Cribyn, Craig Cwareli, Craig Pwllfa, Garn Faw, Upper Neuadd Reservoir

This is a splendid high-level walk with almost 12 miles of the route above 2,000 ft. For most of the way the path follows a cliff edge with a sheer drop and a good head for heights is necessary

Distance: 12 miles
For: Walkers only
Terrain: Difficult
Route-finding: Easy

Maps: 1:25000 Brecon Beacons Outdoor Leisure Map, Central Area; 1:50000 sheet 160
Start: The end of the road at Lower Neuadd Reservoir, grid reference S0032180, 8 miles north of Merthyr Tydfil
Parking: There is limited roadside parking at the start of the walk. There is a Forestry Commission car park ½ mile to the south
Buses: None
Refreshments: None

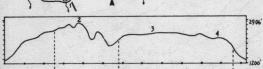

1 Face the reservoir gate, turn left and walk down to two stiles. Cross the stile on the right, ford the stream and walk uphill to a stile in a wire fence near the forest edge. Follow the path alongside the forest and at the top of the ridge turn right. At a junction of tracks, bear right, still following the edge to reach Corn Du and on to Pen y Fan (at 2,906 ft, the highest point in the Brecon Beacons). (*Now turn to p. 70.*)

(*Continued from p. 72*) Aim for the reservoir buildings and cross a broad track to reach the reservoir boundary fence. Turn left and walk to a stile, then turn right and return to your car.

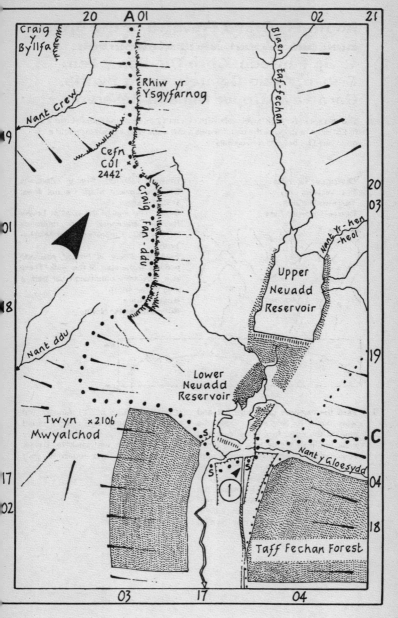

Craig y Byllfa

Nant Crew

Rhiw yr Ysgyfarnog

Cefn Cul 2442'

Craig fan-ddu

Nant ddu

Twyn Mwyalchod ×2106'

Lower Neuadd Reservoir

Upper Neuadd Reservoir

Blaen taf-fechan

Nant yr hen heol

Nant y Gloesydd

Taff Fechan Forest

A 01 02 21

20

20 03

19

19

18

18

C 04

17 02

17

20 01 02

03 17 04

2 Continue following the southern edge (overlooking the reservoir) to Cribyn and then descend to a major crossing of tracks. Bear slightly right to gain a north-facing edge which for the next 2 miles overlooks Brecon.

Continued on p. 72

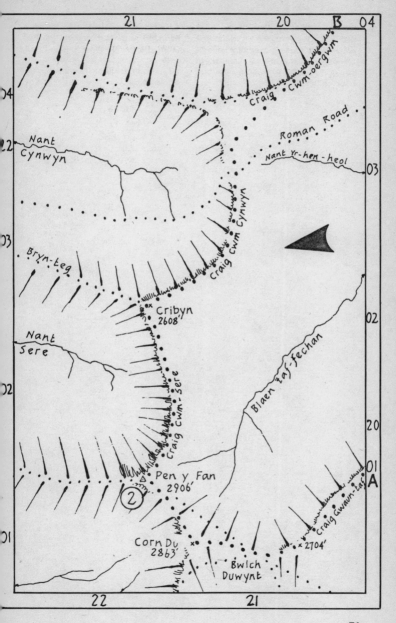

3 At Rhiw Bwlch-y-ddwyalt the edge makes a 90° turn to the right and you will now be looking over a forest with Llangorse Lake in the far distance. In about 1½ miles the edge doubles back on itself.

4 After crossing a stream, take the right-hand fork to the last summit Garn Faw. From the cairn follow the indistinct path aiming towards the forest edge on the other side of the valley. (*Now turn to p. 68.*)

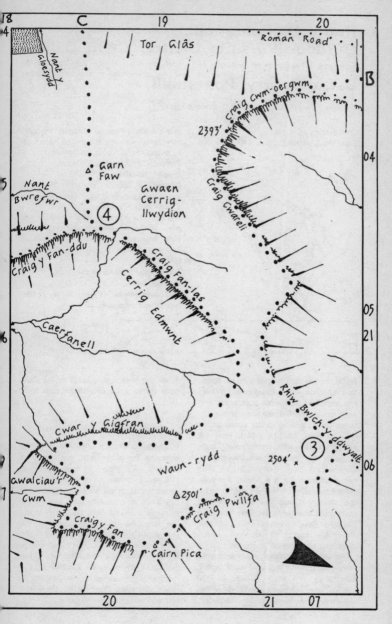

Nant y Gloesydd

Tor Glâs

Roman Road

Craig Cwm-oergwm

2393'

Garn Faw

Gwaen Cerrig-llwydion

Craig Cwareli

Nant Bwrefwr

④

Craig y Fan-ddu

Craig Fan-las

Cerrig Edmwnt

Caerfanell

Rhiw Bwlch-y-ddwyalt

Cwar y Gigfran

③

Waun-rydd

2504' x

Gwalciau'r Cwm

△ 2501'

Craig Pwllfa

Craig y Fan

Cairn Pica

73

Route 12. Pontsticill, Outdoor Pursuits Centre, Cwm Callan, Bryn Cefnog, Baltic Quarry, Pontsticill

A route through forests and into open country

Distance: 9½ miles
For: Walkers and riders. (Riders must

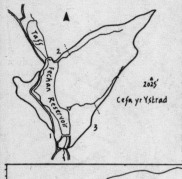

make a short diversion along the road which follows the Pontsticill Reservoir to avoid the stiles in the forest)
Terrain: Moderately difficult
Route-finding: Difficult
Maps: 1:25000 Brecon Beacons Outdoor Leisure Map, Central Area; 1:50000 sheet 160
Start: The Forestry Commission car park on the western side of the Pontsticill Reservoir about 5 miles north of Merthyr Tydfil, grid reference S N057120
Parking: Plentiful at the start
Buses: None
Refreshments: There is a public house in Pontsticill

1 From the car park take the broad forest trail which is waymarked in red. Where the metalled trail ends turn right and walk down the hillside for a short distance until coming to the steep banks of a stream. At this point, turn left along a very narrow path which runs through the forest above the stream. Follow this for a few yards to a wire fence with a stile in it. Cross the stile, walk upstream to the waterfall, cross the stream above the waterfall and make for the stile in the wire fence on the other side. Cross the stile and walk along the broad forest track which gradually becomes metalled. At a point where the two metalled tracks fork, take the left fork and walk uphill. Eventually this track arrives at the road. Turn left and walk downhill ignoring the turning to Talybont,

cross the bridge, and walk to the Outdoor Pursuits Centre. (*Now turn to p. 76.*)

(*Continued from p. 76*) Aim for this, **3** descend the slope, and walk well to the left of a stand of trees. (This is important because of a dangerous, unfenced quarry.) Well to the left of the trees is a square iron gate. Pass through it and follow the path along the left side of a wall until, at the bottom of the hill, it turns sharp right. Here, take the path that goes off to the left towards a white cottage. After 200-300 yds it bears slightly to the right and passes under the railway to reach the road. Turn right, then fork left and walk to the car park.

74

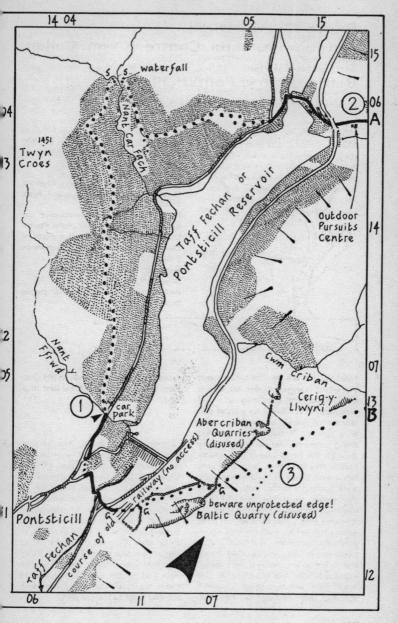

waterfall

Nant Cat fach

Twyn Croes
1451

Taff Fechan or Pontsticill Reservoir

Outdoor Pursuits Centre

Nant y Ffrwd

car park

① ▲

Cwm criban

Cerig-y-Llwyni

Abercriban Quarries (disused)

③

railway (no access)

beware unprotected edge!
Baltic Quarry (disused)

Pontsticill

Taff Fechan

course of old

② A

B

14 04   05   15

04

13

12

05

07

11

11   07

06

75

2   At the Outdoor Pursuits Centre the metalling ceases and the surface deteriorates into a track. Pass through three gates and cross a culvert before reaching Blaencallan Farm, which is now a ruin. Follow the conifer plantation on the right to reach a gate in a wire fence which gives access to open country. Cross a tiny stream, turn right and take the clearly defined track which soon turns into a grassy path. After about a mile the path reaches an edge, overlooking a valley. Take the path to the right. On reaching a boggy patch the path bends sharply left. Follow the edge of the bog and aim a little to the right of the quarry. Cross two roads and then follow the main road into the quarry workings. A little way along it, bear off to the right. At a point where the road bears round to the left leave the road and bear right to follow the clearly defined path which follows for 100 yds or so the left side of the stream. Continue until the stream bears round to the right towards the reservoir. At this point, after passing a very wide grassy area, bear left and follow the path that goes up the hillside. Near the top it tends to peter out, but keep well up on the left-hand side of the flank of the hill and on reaching the top you will see in the far distance a white circular estate of houses. (*Now turn to p. 74.*)

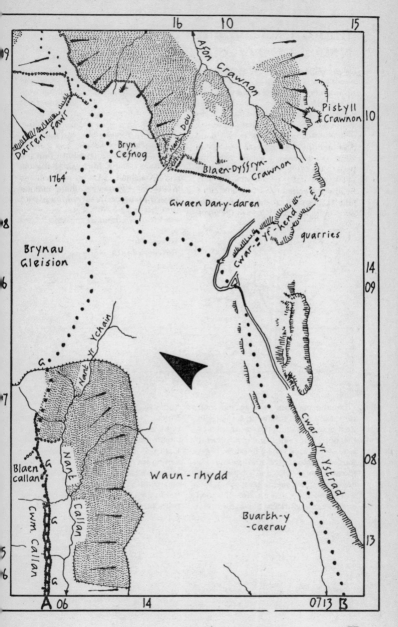

The map contains the following labels:

16 · 10 · 15

Afon Crawnon

Darren-fawr

Pistyll Crawnon

Bryn Cefnog

Nant Dou

Blaen-Dyffryn-Crawnon

1764'

Gwaen Dan-y-daren

Brynau Gleision

Cwar-yr-hend- quarries

14
09

Nant yr Ychain

G

Nant yr Ychain

Cwar yr Ystrad

Blaen callan

Waun-rhydd

Nant Callan

G

Buarth-y-caerau

08

Cwm Callan

G

13

G

A 06 · 14 · 0713 B

Route 13. Talybont Forest, Neuadd Reservoir, Craig Pwllfa, Talybont Forest

A splendid high-level route with superb views

Distance: 11 miles
For: Walkers only

Terrain: Difficult
Route-finding: Easy
Maps: 1:25000 Brecon Beacons Outdoor Leisure Map, Central Area; 1:50000 sheet 161
Start: The Forestry Commission car park 8 miles north of Merthyr Tydfil, grid reference S N056175
Parking: Plentiful at the start of the walk
Buses: None
Refreshments: None

1   From the car park walk to the road, turn right and follow it for ½ mile. Just before meeting the forest edge on the right, turn right along a metalled lane which quickly deteriorates. Take the right-hand fork and follow the forest edge. At the end of the forest, pass through a gate and continue forward. The track just touches the road and then immediately bears right by a notice which says 'Unsuitable for Motors'. Follow the forest edge on the right and then descend to cross a stream running in a deep channel. Continue forward past the reservoir, aiming for the pass ahead where there is a major junction of paths. Turn right and climb a very steep path towards the summit and then take the path that bears off to the right.

Continued on p. 80

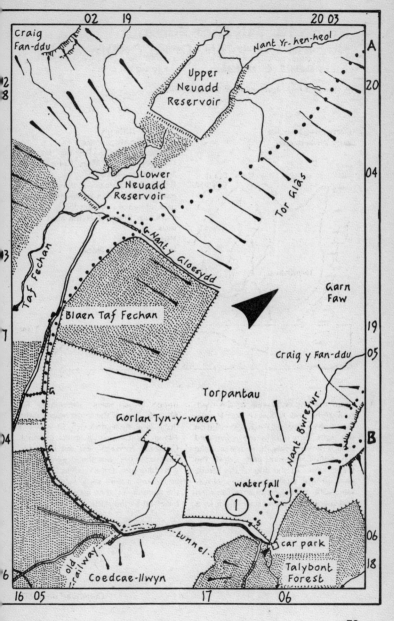

Craig
Fan-ddu

Nant Yr-hen-heol

Upper
Neuadd
Reservoir

Lower
Neuadd
Reservoir

Tor Glas

Nant y Gloesydd

Taf Fechan

Blaen Taf Fechan

Garn
Faw

Craig y Fan-ddu

Torpantau

Gorlan Tyn-y-waen

Nant Bwrefwr

waterfall

①

tunnel

car park

old railway

Coedcae-llwyn

Talybont
Forest

A

20

04

19

05

B

06

18

02   19   20 03

16 05   17   06

2 At the top of the ridge follow the edge which overlooks Brecon and the Usk Valley keeping the edge on the left. Follow the edge for about 4 miles at a height of about 2,500 ft. It doubles back on itself and then heads due south. Descend the steep saddle towards the forest. Cross the stream and follow the path to a stile. Turn left and walk to the car park.

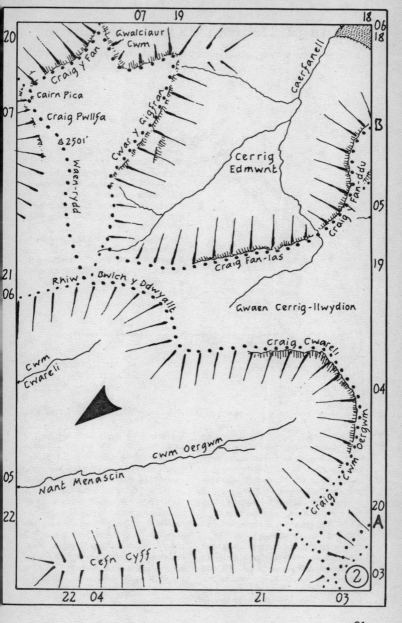

Route 14. Llanfrynach and the Beacons

A fine and remarkably easy route which climbs to 2,500 ft and offers splendid views

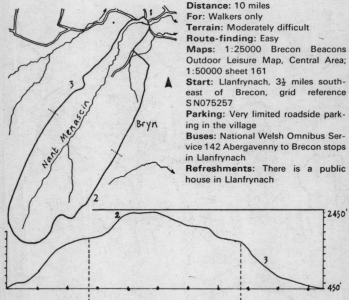

Distance: 10 miles
For: Walkers only
Terrain: Moderately difficult
Route-finding: Easy
Maps: 1:25000 Brecon Beacons Outdoor Leisure Map, Central Area; 1:50000 sheet 161
Start: Llanfrynach, 3½ miles south-east of Brecon, grid reference SN075257
Parking: Very limited roadside parking in the village
Buses: National Welsh Omnibus Service 142 Abergavenny to Brecon stops in Llanfrynach
Refreshments: There is a public house in Llanfrynach

1   From the road junction on the eastern side of the church, take the road that bears to the left and crosses the river. Shortly afterwards turn right along a lane with a 'No Through Road' sign and after 700 yds turn left into a gated, unmetalled, enclosed track. Follow this through a gate and drop down to a ford. Go on along a track enclosed with old trees until level with a farm. *Do not go through the gate ahead* but turn right and walk through a gate into the wood. Immediately turn left and follow the fence which marks the boundary of the wood. At the top of the wood turn right and keep inside the boundary fence until reaching a gate. Pass through it and continue forward up the steep hill on a broad, grassy path to a wood. Walk round the outside of the wood, ignoring any paths on the left. At the end of the wood, bear left and contour the hill. *Do not climb to the top but follow the path which climbs steadily over the shoulder until it emerges on top of a grassy weald.* Ahead is a large mountain and the path can clearly be seen going over its right flank. Follow the path all the way to the top of the cwm.

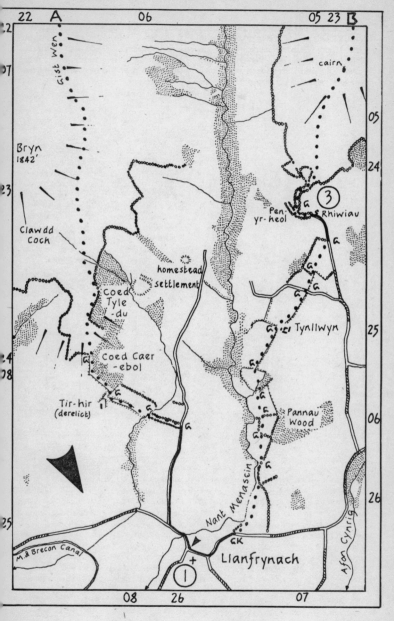

22   A   06   05 23 B

Cist Wen

cairn

Bryn
1842'

Clawdd
Coch

homestead
settlement

Coed
Tyle
-du

Pen-
yr-heol   ③ Rhiwiau

Coed Caer
-ebol

Tynllwyn

Tir-hir
(derelict)

Pannau
Wood

Nant Menascin

M.ª Brecon Canal

CK

+   Llanfrynach

①

Afon Cynrig

08   26   07

83

2   Follow the precipitous edge (but not too close!) to reach a large cairn with the Upper Neuadd Reservoir below on the left. Take the path that bears off to the right and descends a ridge past several cairns. After about three miles the path drops down very steeply to a stone wall. Bear right and go through a gate into an enclosed track. Near the bottom of this stony track pass through a gate and turn left to reach a metalled lane.

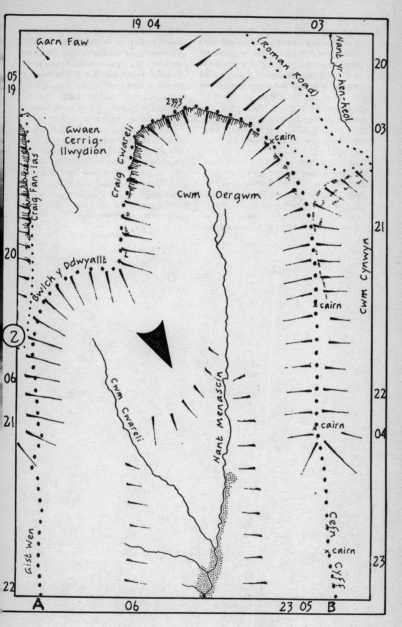

Garn Faw

19 04   03

(Roman Road)

Nant yr-hen-heol

05
19

20

03

2393'

Gwaen
Cerrig-
llwydion

Craig Fan-las

Craig Cwareli

Cwm   Oergwm

x cairn

21

Bwlch y Ddwyallt

20

Cwm Cynwyn

② 2

x cairn

Cwm Cwareli

Nant Menascin

06

21

22

x cairn

04

04

Gist Wen

Cefn Cyff

x cairn

23

A   06   23 05   B

22

85

3   Follow the lane past several houses. After passing the last house on the right either follow the road into Llanfrynach or take the gate on the right-hand side of the road, and walk diagonally across the field (parallel to the wood) to a gate. Pass through the gate and walk down the right-hand headland to a gate which gives access to a minor road. Cross the road, take the gate opposite and walk down the left-hand headland to Tynllwyn Farm and an enclosed lane. Turn right, pass through a waymarked gate, turn left and walk down the headland of the field. Pass through a waymarked gate, bear very slightly left and aim for the waymark on the tree clearly visible ahead. At the waymark, follow a farm track, with a stream on the left-hand side. At the bottom of the next field, pass through a waymarked gate on the left, cross the stream which you have been following and aim for the waymarked gate ahead. Follow the bank of the stream for a short distance until emerging into a flat grassy field. Cross the field following the waymarks, take a track which climbs upwards and after a few yards emerges into another field and make for the gate ahead by the waymark. Pass through the waymarked gate into a wet sunken lane which emerges into a field. Follow the river's edge all the way to a gate and kissing gate at the road. Turn right and walk down to Llanfrynach.

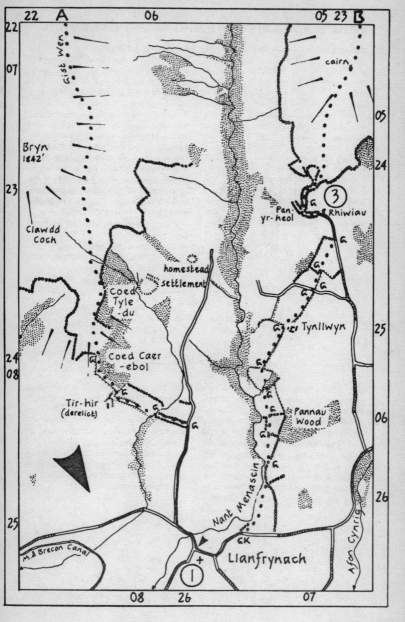

A   22   06   05   23   B

22

07

cairn

05

Gist Wen

Bryn
1842'

24

Clawdd
Coch

23

Pen-
yr-heol

Rhiwiau

③

homestead
settlement

Coed
Tyle
-du

Tynllwyn

25

24
08

Coed Caer
-ebol

Tir-hir
(derelict)

Pannau
Wood

06

Nant Menascin

25

Afon Cynrig

26

M.& Brecon Canal

CK

Llanfrynach

①

+

08   26   07

Route 15. Talybont and Cwm Crawnon

An easy route through forests along tracks and a canal towpath

Distance: 8½ miles
For: Walkers only

Terrain: Easy
Route-finding: Easy
Maps: 1:25000 Brecon Beacons Outdoor Leisure Map, Central Area; 1:50000 sheet 161
Start: Talybont, about one mile south of the A40 midway between Brecon and Crickhowell, grid reference SN115225
Parking: Roadside parking in Talybont
Buses: National Welsh Omnibus Service 142 Abergavenny to Brecon stops at Talybont
Refreshments: Two public houses in Talybont

1 Take the steeply rising track which goes up the right-hand side of the White Hart Inn and crosses the canal. It then bears right, levels out and turns left to cross the old railway by a bridge and then turns right and enters the forest. Just inside the forest, fork left and, about 1½ miles later, fork left again. About ½ mile beyond the second fork, a path crosses the track. Turn left and walk steeply uphill for 100 yds to reach a gate which gives access to open country.

Continue forward along a path which moves slightly away from the forest on the left to reach a road opposite the track which leads to Bwlch-y-Waun Farm. Follow the track through several gates to reach a road about a mile after passing the farm. **2**

Continued on p. 90

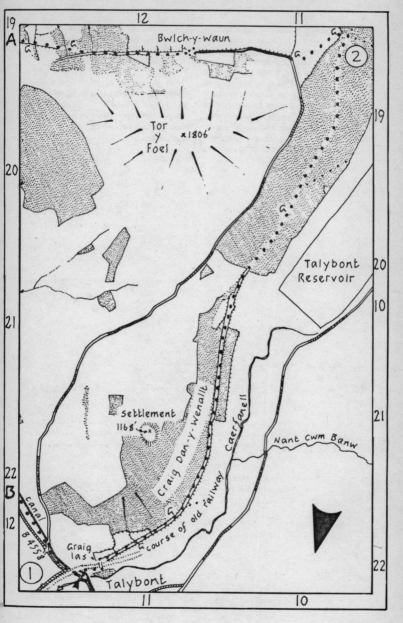

At the road, turn left and then right at the next farm, following a track between the farm and cottage to reach a gate. Bear slightly left and pass through a gate and, keeping the hedge on the left, walk down to a stone stile and then aim for the gate by the farm ahead. Cross the road to a gate and cross the field diagonally to pass through the gate on the left of a pair. Continue diagonally past a telegraph pole to reach a stile and on to the next stile in the far left-hand corner of the field. Continue forward to another stile and the path descends steeply to the canal locks.

Cross the canal, turn left and follow the towpath all the way to bridge 143. Turn right to reach the bank of the White Hart Inn. (There is no towpath through the tunnel but the route is signposted.)

3

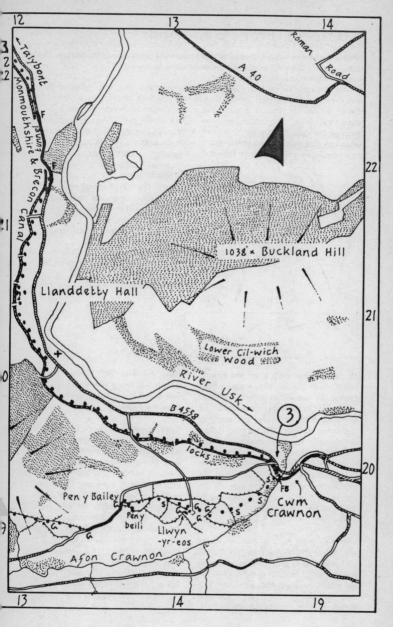

12   13   14

Talybont

Monmouthshire & Brecon Canal

Taf Fawr

F

F

22

21

1038 × Buckland Hill

Llanddetty Hall

X

Lower Cil-wich Wood

River Usk

B 4558

③

locks

20

Pen y Bailey

Peny beili

S

S

S

S

G

G

S

FB

Cwm Crawnon

G

G

Llwyn -yr-eos

Afon Crawnon

13   14   19

91

Route 16. From Llangynidr

This is a desolate walk across wild and featureless country and should be attempted only by those competent with map and compass

Distance: 5½ miles
For: Walkers only

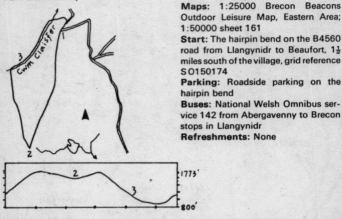

Terrain: Difficult
Route-finding: Difficult
Maps: 1:25000 Brecon Beacons Outdoor Leisure Map, Eastern Area; 1:50000 sheet 161
Start: The hairpin bend on the B4560 road from Llangynidr to Beaufort, 1½ miles south of the village, grid reference SO150174
Parking: Roadside parking on the hairpin bend
Buses: National Welsh Omnibus service 142 from Abergavenny to Brecon stops in Llangynidr
Refreshments: None

1 Ignore the gated track on the hairpin bend and follow the path which climbs the hillside moving away from the track. On reaching the edge of the forest, turn left and climb to the top of the stone outcrop. Turn right, follow the outcrop for a short distance and then follow the path marked by a few posts which goes off to the left. The path passes a little to the left of the trig point and then peters out. At the trig point take a compass bearing of 207°. Walk on this bearing for 1¼ miles.

2 You will then pass a pool of water about 200 yds off the route on the left and about 300 yds later you should reach a small circular quarry. Walk on for about another 100 yds and you may be able to make out a narrow, indistinct path. Follow this path (compass bearing 355°) for 1½ miles which will bring you to a steep sided valley (on the right a spring bubbles from the hillside).

Cross the stream near a waterfall, turn **3** right and follow the stream past some waterworks. Cross the wire fence and pass some ruined buildings and then keep to the path between the stream and the forest. Here and there are the remains of an old enclosed track. When this track bears off to the left, leave it, pass through some farm buildings and follow a farm track through a series of gates, past a ruined dutch barn. It then bears off to the right, crosses a ford and reaches the road at a gate. Turn right, cross the bridge and follow the road all the way to the main road. Turn right and walk back to your car.

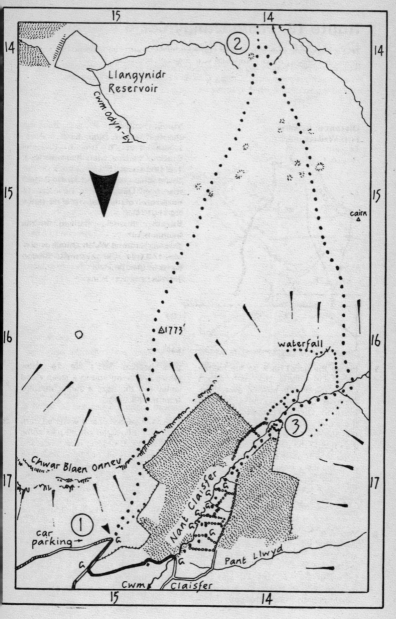

Llangynidr
Reservoir

Cwm Odyn-fy

②

cairn

Δ1773'

waterfall

③

Chwar Blaen Onney

Nant Claisfer

car parking →

①

Pant Llwyd

Cwm Claisfer

14

15

16

17

15

14

Route 17. Llangattock, Craig y Cilau, Cwm Onneu, Llangattock

A short but very demanding route, involving a steep climb and the negotiation of a precipitous scree slope. Craig y Cilau is a National Nature Reserve containing some rare white hornbeams

Distance: 5 miles
For: Walkers only
Terrain: Difficult
Route-finding: Difficult

Maps: 1:25000 Brecon Beacons Outdoor Leisure Map, Eastern Area; 1:50000 sheet 161
Start: The sharp left-hand bend ½ mile south-west of Llangattock on the unclassified road to Llanelly, grid reference SO206169
Parking: Very limited roadside parking at the start of the walk
Buses: National Welsh Omnibus Company service 142 Brecon to Abergavenny stops near Llangattock on the southern side of Crickhowell bridge
Refreshments: Public house in Llangattock

1 Cross the stile beside the gate which leads into the enclosed, disused tramway track. Follow the track past a house and across a stream to a field. Bear right and follow the headland and then climb a fence and walk up the steep incline beside a conifer plantation. At the top of the incline, bear slightly left and follow the path towards the escarpment.

2 Just below the cliffs, turn right and follow the clear path into the Craig y Cilau National Nature Reserve, famous for its rare trees, and past the Agen Allwedd cave system which stretches for 18 miles inside the mountain. The entrance is guarded by an unobtrusive iron door beside the path. Soon the path narrows and climbs across a scree, with a tremendous drop below, to reach the top of the cliffs. Follow the top of the cliffs until the path

drops down a surprisingly easy descent to reach a wide track.

Turn right and follow the track but do **3** not actually touch the nearby road. Instead, continue forward to reach a track running downhill beside a stone wall. Nearby is the Craig y Cilau National Nature Reserve notice board. As the steep slope is descended to the flat field aim for the low stone wall which crosses the stream. Follow the right-hand side of this wall, cross the stream and follow the wall. Where it bends sharply left follow it to a stream and a gate, continue forward for a few yards and then pass through a gate on the right. Follow the clear path through a number of fields to reach a stile on the edge of a wood. Cross the stile and then leave the clear path which climbs up through the wood and, instead, follow the wire fence on

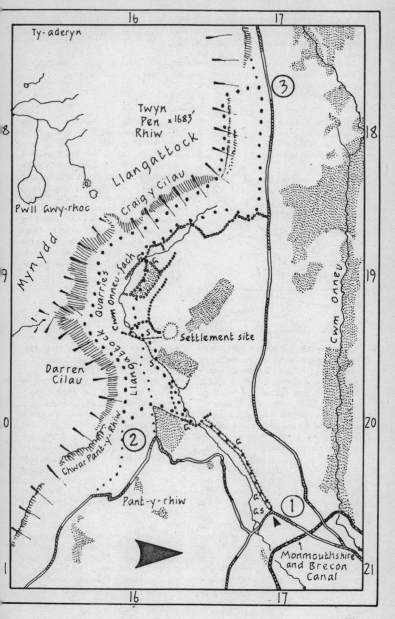

Ty-aderyn

16

17

③

Twyn
Pen ×1683′
Rhiw

Llangattock

8

18

Craig y Cilau

Pwll Gwy-rhoc

Quarries

Mynydd

Cwm Onneu-fach

9

19

Settlement site

Cwm Onneu

Darren
Cilau

Llangattock

②

Chwar Pant-y-rhiw

0

20

Pant-y-rhiw

①

G
Gs

Monmouthshire
and Brecon
Canal

1

21

16

17

your right to reach a rudimentary stile in the fence. Cross the stile and the stream and then turn left and follow a narrow path which will bring you back to the bottom of the steep incline near the start of the walk. Return to your car.

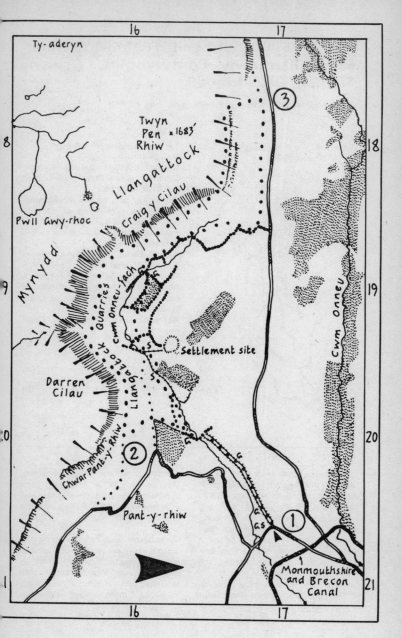

Ty-aderyn

Twyn
Pen ×1683'
Rhiw

③

Llangattock

Craig y Cilau

8

18

Pwll Gwy-rhoc

Mynydd

Quarries

Cwm Onneu-fach

9

19

Settlement site

Cwm Onneu

Darren
Cilau

Llangáttock

②

20

20

Chwar Pant-y-rhiw

①

Pant-y-rhiw

Monmouthshire
and Brecon
Canal

21

16

17

Route 18. Crickhowell, Table Mountain, Pen Allt-mawr, Pentwynglas, Grwyne Fechan, Crickhowell

A route following well-used paths which climb to 2,360 ft

Distance: 12½ miles
For: Walkers only

Terrain: Moderately difficult
Route-finding: Easy
Maps: 1:25000 Brecon Beacons Outdoor Leisure Map, Eastern Area; 1:50000 sheet 161
Start: Car park on the Abergavenny side of Crickhowell just off the A40, grid reference S N219184
Parking: There is a large car park at the start of the walk
Buses: Cross Gates Motors Service 360 Llandrindod Wells to Cardiff. Williams' Coaches Service 387 Talgarth to Abergavenny and the Welsh National Omnibus Service 142 stop at Crickhowell
Refreshments: Plentiful in Crickhowell

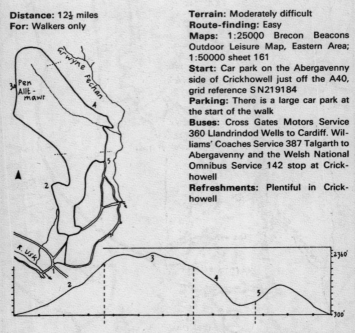

1 From the car park walk back to the road and then turn left and walk uphill. At the top, turn right and then left into Great Oak Road. About 300 yds beyond a road junction, turn left along an enclosed track opposite an electricity substation and just below a metalled farm lane. After ¼ mile turn right along an enclosed path which climbs uphill and meets a track at a T-junction. Turn left and follow the track through a gate and into a steep-sided wooded valley. The track goes uphill parallel to, but some distance above, the stream. At a gate the path continues forward following the bed of a stream and after a short distance is enclosed with walls.

On reaching open country follow the 2 general direction of the wall on the right ignoring paths which go off to the left. On a saddle to the left of Table Mountain turn left along a grassy track for about 3 miles, always keeping to the highest ground.

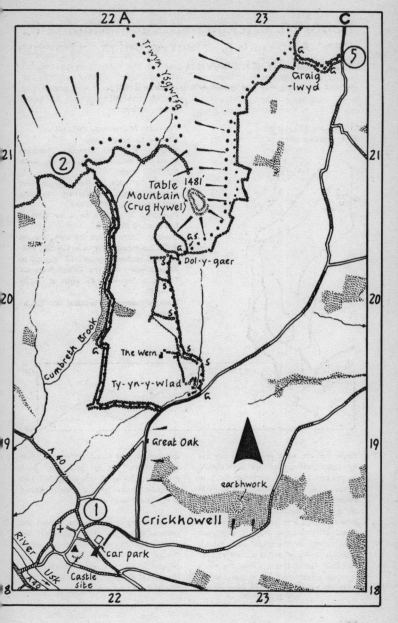

22 A · · · 23 C

Trwyn Ysgwrfa

⑤

Craig
-lwyd

②

Table 1481'
Mountain
(Crug Hywel)

Gs.
G
Dol-y-gaer

S
S
S

Cumbreth Brook

G
The Wern S
S
Ty-yn-y-wlad G

Great Oak

earthwork

① Crickhowell

+

car park

River

Castle
site

Usk
A 40

22 23

There is a trig point on Pen Cerrig-calch (2,300 ft) and another on Pen Allt-mawr (2,360 ft).

3 The path still keeps to the highest ground and tends to bear right to reach Pentwynglas, where there are some nineteenth-century boundary stones. From the summit look back towards Pen Allt-mawr and observe the junction of paths below you. Take the left-hand fork, which at first is quite faint but as soon as it starts to descend the other side of the hill becomes much clearer and finally becomes a track. It passes several old quarries and then reaches enclosed country at a gate.

Continued on p. 102

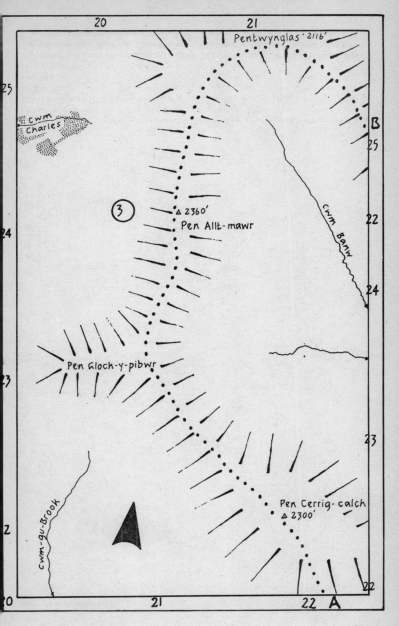

Pentwynglas 2116'

cwm
Charles

③

△ 2360'
Pen Allt-mawr

cwm Banw

Pen Gloch-y-pibwr

Pen Cerrig-calch
△ 2300'

cwm-gu-Brook

B

A

4 Continue forward through a series of gates until reaching a road at Neuadd Fawr Farm. Turn right and follow the road round a hairpin bend until, after about a mile, reaching a cottage and a sign 'Footpath only' on the right.

Continued on p. 104

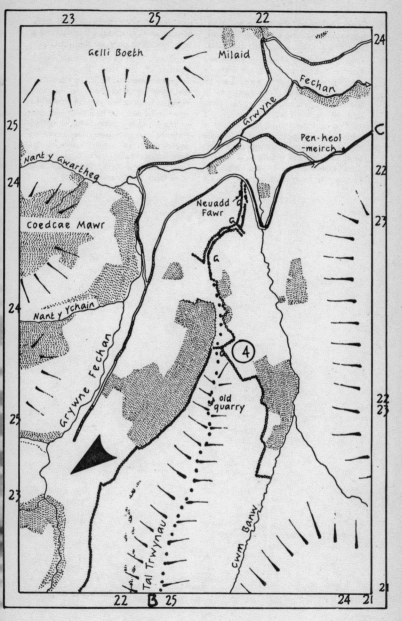

Gelli Boeth

Milaid

Fechan

Grwyne

Pen-heol
-meirch

Nant y Gwartheg

Coedcae Mawr

Neuadd
Fawr

Nant y Ychain

Grwyne Fechan

④

old
quarry

Tal Trwynau

Cwm Banw

5   Follow the enclosed path uphill passing through a gate by a ruined building to reach open country at a gate. Bear slightly right, continue uphill and after about 50 yds turn left along a broad grassy path which runs parallel to the wall below. Fork right near a triangular section of wall, and continue forward with the wall about 100 yds on the left. Ignore all paths which run off the main path. Shortly after passing some straggly pine trees on the left a broad grassy path sweeps down from the top of Table Mountain. Follow the path to a gate and walk down an enclosed track. Pass through the next gate, immediately turn left over a stile and walk down the left-hand headland to meet a track at the bottom of the field. Bear left and follow the enclosed track to a gate. *Do not pass through the gate* but turn right, cross a stile and walk down the left-hand headland to a gate and stile at the bottom of the field. Continue forward to a gate giving access to an enclosed track which should be followed across a stile to a gate at the road beside a farm. Turn right and walk back to Crickhowell.

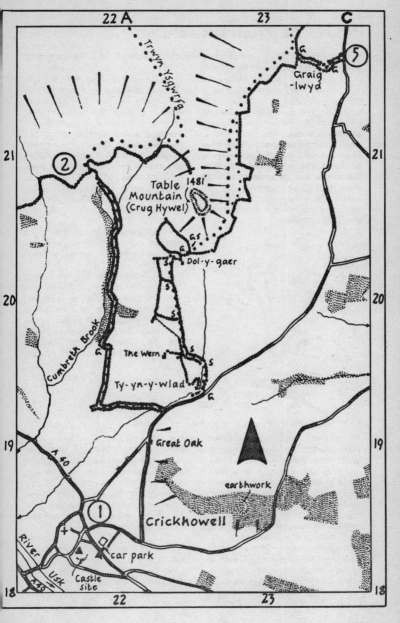

22 A   23   C

Trwyn Ysgwrfa

⑤

Graig -lwyd

21

②

21

Table Mountain (Crug Hywel) 1481

GS

G

Dol-y-gaer

20

Cumbeth Brook

20

S

S

S

The Wern S

S

Ty-yn-y-wlad G

Great Oak

19

A 40

19

earthwork

Crickhowell

①

car park

River

Usk

A 40

Castle site

18

22   23

18

Route 19. From Cwmdu

A route across fields and well-marked tracks climbing to 1,500 ft. There are splendid views across Llangorse Lake

Distance: 7 miles
For: Walkers and riders. (Riders must make a slight detour at the beginning to avoid the direct footpath from Cwmdu, using the lanes to join the route near Llwynau-mawr. The descent at (3) on the map is very steep and riders may have to dismount and lead their horses)

Terrain: Moderately difficult
Route-finding: Easy
Maps: 1:25000 Brecon Beacons Outdoor Leisure Map, Eastern Area; 1:50000 sheet 161
Start: Lay-by on the A479 in the hamlet of Cwmdu, 4 miles north-west of Crickhowell, grid reference SN180237
Parking: Limited parking in lay-by at start of walk. More is available just north of Cwmdu in lay-by on main road
Buses: Cross Gates Motors Service 360 Llandrindod Wells to Cardiff, and Williams' Coaches Service 387 Talgarth to Abergavenny, stop at Cwmdu
Refreshments: Small public house in Cwmdu. The public house at Tretower, 1½ miles south of Cwmdu, serves bar snacks

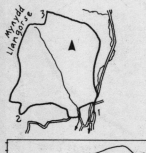

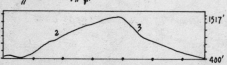

1   At the central crossroads in Cwmdu walk down the hill along the road that leads away from the church. Cross a stone bridge, ignore a gate which leads to the farm drive and take the gate on the right a few yards further along the road. Take the wide track and make for the gate ahead. Pass through this and continue across the next field to another gate. Pass through this and continue in the same direction to a gate which brings you to the road. At the road turn left and at the T-junction turn right. At the first farm turn right and enter an enclosed roughly metalled track. Fork left

through a gate to reach Pen-yr-heol Farm. Pass through the farmyard, turn right and climb steeply uphill, keeping a stone wall on the left. Near the top, climb a hurdle and follow the stone wall round to the left to reach a gate. Pass through it into an enclosed track. At Crindau, the path is metalled and should be followed to a gate.

Shortly after passing the ruin on the   **2** left there is a junction of tracks by a cattle trough. Turn sharp right and go by a roughly walled track up the hill. 200 yds after leaving the barbed-wire fence is a crossing of paths. Bear

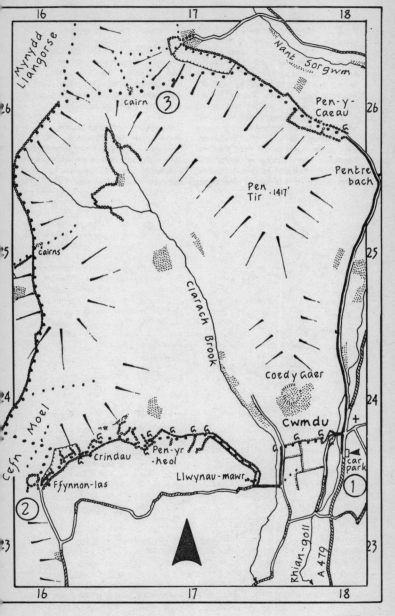

Mynydd Llangorse

cairn ③

Pen-y-Caeau

Nant Sorgwm

Pen Tir ·1417'

Pentre bach

cairns

Clarach Brook

Coed y Gaer

Cwmdu +

car park ►

①

Cefn Moel

Crindau

Pen-yr -heol

Llwynau-mawr

Ffynnon-las

②

Rhian-goll

A 479

16   17   18

slightly right and follow a broad grassy track. *Do not take the path that goes towards the isolated tree on your left.* Follow the broad grassy path which ultimately narrows until it reaches a stone wall. Turn right and follow a broad track for ¾ mile to a cairn where a path crosses. Continue forward for ½ mile to a boundary stone. (The Ordnance Survey map does not show the broad path swinging away northwards but only the bridleway that bears round to the right.) At the boundary stone continue on for another 200 yds and then take the grassy path which strikes off to the right.

Here you can see down the valley and this should be done to confirm your position. Follow the clear path until almost reaching a cairn. Bear left, pass close to the cairn and head in a north-east direction until reaching the escarpment. The Ordnance Survey map wrongly shows the path going down the sheer escarpment.

Instead turn right and follow a much wider path which bears left and gradually drops down the escarpment. Turn right and follow a track through a series of gates to a metalled lane and the main road at Cwmdu.

3

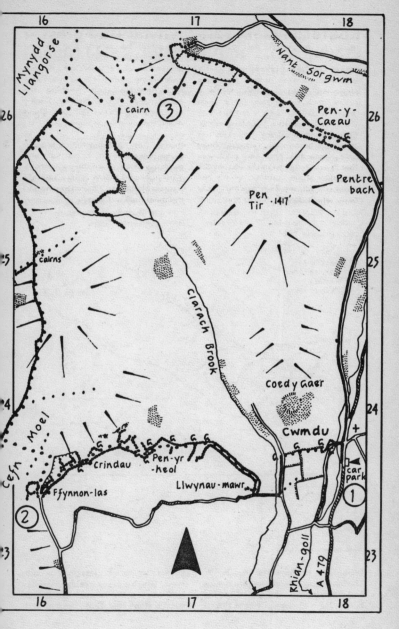

Route 20. Llanbedr, Mynydd Du Forest, Waun Fach, Pen Allt-mawr, Table Mountain, Llanbedr

A superb high-level route, much of it above the 2,000-ft contour

Distance: 17 miles
For: Walkers and riders. (Riders must make a short diversion along the road from Llanbedr to Draen to avoid the footpath to Hen-bant)
Terrain: Moderately difficult
Route-finding: Easy
Maps: 1:25000 Brecon Beacons Outdoor Leisure Map, Eastern Area; 1:50000 sheet 161

Start: Llanbedr, 2 miles north-east of Crickhowell, grid reference S N239204
Parking: Limited roadside parking at the road junction ¼ mile west of Llanbedr, grid reference S N234203
Buses: Williams' Coaches Service 390 from Llanbedr to Abergavenny
Refreshments: None

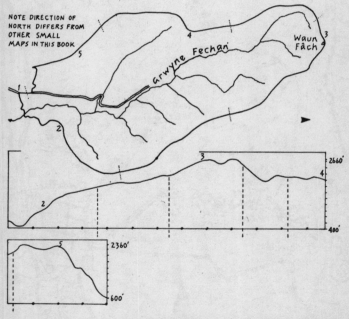

NOTE DIRECTION OF NORTH DIFFERS FROM OTHER SMALL MAPS IN THIS BOOK

1 Walk down the lane past the church. The lane soon deteriorates into a track and drops down to the river. Cross the bridge, leave the obvious track beside the river and take the less obvious path ahead which zigzags steeply upwards. Half way up the hillside, fork left to reach a stone stile. Cross the stile and

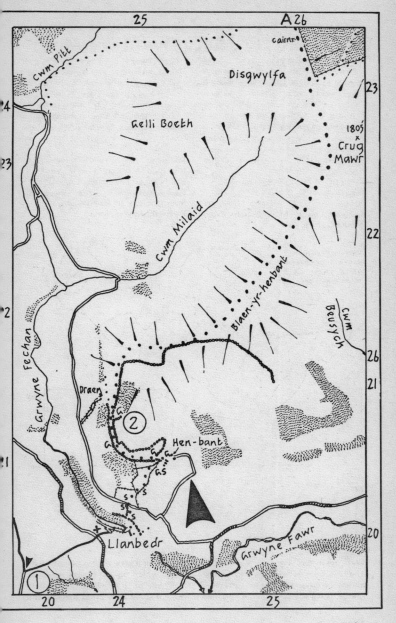

A26

cairn

Disgwylfa

Cwm Pitt

Gelli Boeth

Cwm Milaid

1805
x
Crug
Mawr

Blaen-yr-henbant

Cwm Beusych

Grwyne Fechan

Draen

(2)

Hen-bant

GS

GS

S

S

S

Llanbedr

Grwyne Fawr

(1)

25   A26

23

22

26

21

20

4

23

2

1

20   24   25

111

continue forward along the headland to a stone stile at the road. Cross the road and make for the stone stile in the top right-hand corner of the field. Now aim to the left of the farm and walk to a gate and a stile. Continue forward to pass the farm and reach a gate. At the gate, turn left and pass through another gate which gives access to an enclosed track which should be followed until reaching open country.

At the gate at the end of the enclosed track, bear right and follow the path which runs roughly parallel to the wall on the right for about $\frac{1}{4}$ mile. The path bears to the left, climbs to the top of a ridge and then runs along the forest edge.

2

Continued on p 114

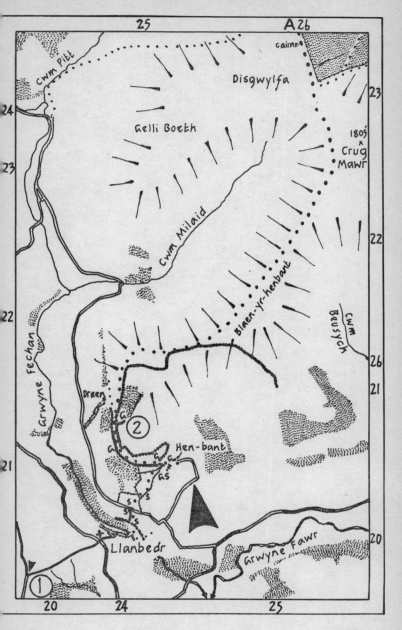

cwm Pill

A 26

cairns

Disgwylfa

Gelli Boeth

Cwm Milaid

1805
x
Crug
Mawr

Blaen-yr-henbant

Cwm Beusych

Grwyne Fechan

Draen

②

Hen-bant

Llanbedr

Grwyne Fawr

①

Follow the clear path along the edge
of Mynydd Du Forest.

Continued on p. 116

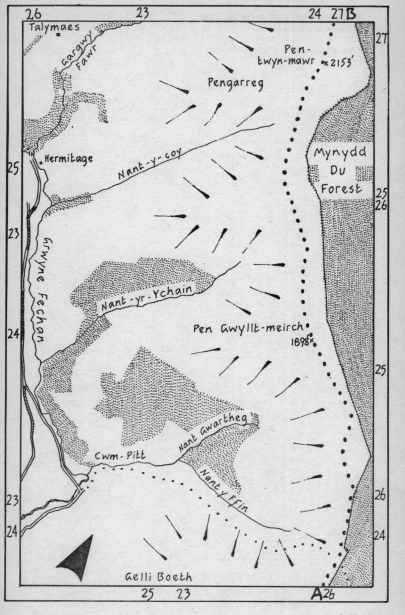

26 23 24 27 B
27

Talymaes
Gargwy Fawr
Pen-twyn-mawr x 2153'
Pengarreg
Hermitage
Nant-y-coy
Mynydd Du Forest
25
26

Grwyne Fechan

Nant-yr-Ychain

Pen Gwyllt-meirch
1898 x

Nant Gwartheg

Cwm-Pitt
Nant y Ffin

Gelli Boeth
25 23 A 26

When the forest ends continue along the path on the summit of the ridge past Pen y Gadair Fawr to reach the base of the old trig point on Waun Fach. Here bear slightly left and follow the path to Pen Trumau keeping the valley on the left.

Continued on p. 118

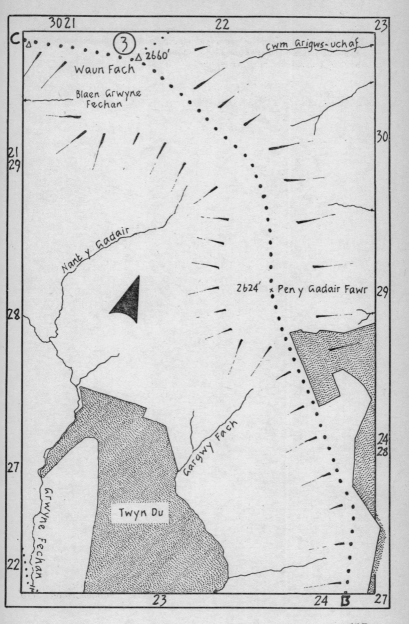

3021   22   23

C

③

cwm Grigws-uchaf

△ 2660'

Waun Fach

Blaen Grwyne Fechan

30

Nant y Gadair

21
29

2624' × Pen y Gadair Fawr

29

28

Gargwy Fach

24
28

27

Grwyne Fechan

Twyn Du

22

23   24   B   27

3 From Pen Trumau follow the steeply sloping ridge to a junction of paths at a cairn. Continue forward heading for the ridge of Mynydd Llysiau and then follow the ridge keeping to the highest ground.

Continued on p. 120

118

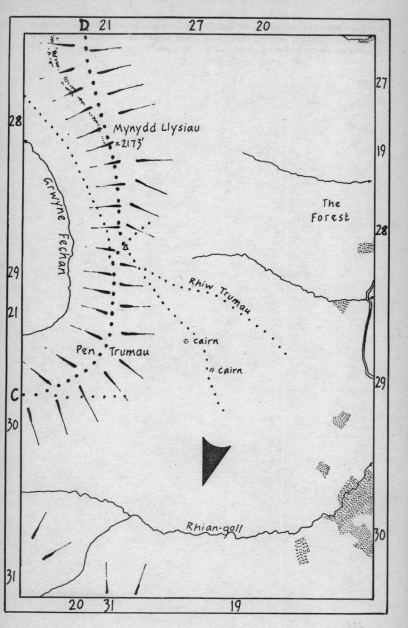

D 21   27   20

27

Mynydd Llysiau
×2173′

Grwyne Fechan

28

19

The
Forest

28

29

21

Rhiw Trumau

cairn

cairn

Pen · Trumau

29

C

30

Rhian-goll

30

31

20   31   19

4 From Mynydd Llysiau keep to the high ground until reaching the old boundary stones on Pentwynglas. Note the junction of paths below. Take the more obvious path which forks right and climbs to the top of Pen Allt-mawr and on to Pen Cerrig-calch.

Continued on p. 122

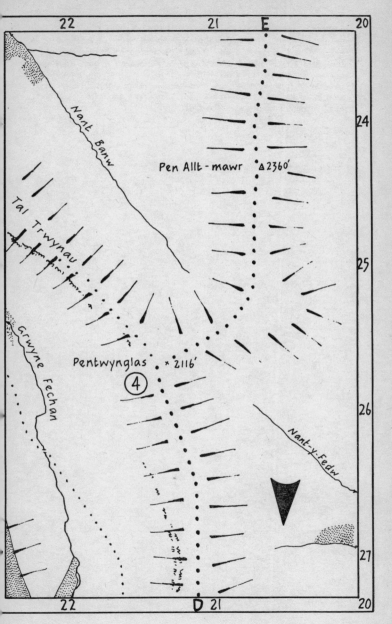

Nant Banw

Pen Allt - mawr △ 2360'

Tal Trwynau

Grwyne Fechan

Pentwynglas × 2116'

④

Nant-y-Fedw

5 From Pen Allt-mawr, follow the high ground to Pen Cerrig-calch and then descend the ridge towards Table Mountain. From Table Mountain, turn left and follow the path down to a gate. Walk forward down the headland, pass a stone barn on the left to reach a gap. Pass through the gap, turn right and follow the path diagonally right across the field. At the end of the field turn left and follow the track to a gate, turn right and follow the enclosed track downhill to a stile and footpath sign at a road. Turn right and walk to Llanbedr.

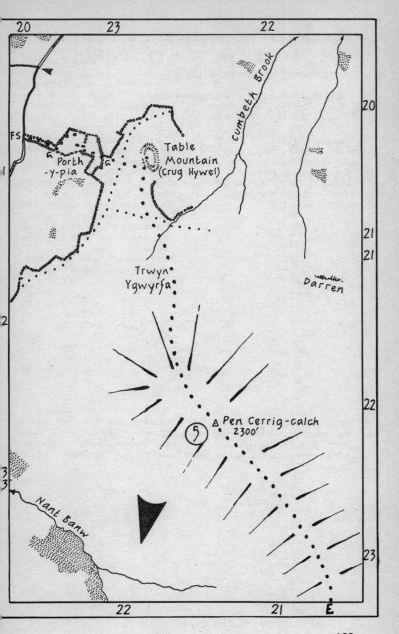

20   23   22

Cumbeth Brook

20

FS

Porth
-y-pia

Table
Mountain
(Crug Hywel)

21

21

Trwyn
Ygwyrfa

Darren

22

△ Pen Cerrig-calch
2300'

⑤

3
3

Nant Banw

23

22   21   E

Route 21. Pengenfford, Y Grib, Pen y Manllwyn, Waun Fach, Pen Trumau, Pengenfford

A fine high-level route with superb views

Distance: 7½ miles
For: Walkers and riders
Terrain: Moderately difficult
Route-finding: Easy
Maps: 1:25000 Brecon Beacons Outdoor Leisure Map, Eastern Area; 1:50000 sheet 161

Start: The telephone box at Pengenfford, grid reference SO173301, at the highest point on the A479, 3 miles south of Talgarth
Parking: Roadside parking beside the telephone box
Buses: A very limited service to Pengenfford operated by Cross Gates Motors (Penybont to Cardiff) and Williams' Coaches (Talgarth to Abergavenny)
Refreshments: The Castle Inn, ¼ mile south of the start of the walk

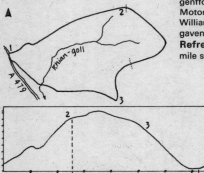

1   Follow the track on the right of the telephone box to the road. Turn left, continue to where the metalling ceases, turn right and follow the track through a gate into open country. Follow the grassy path up the obvious ridge and continue along ridge for 2 miles to Pen y Manllwyn.

Continued on p. 126

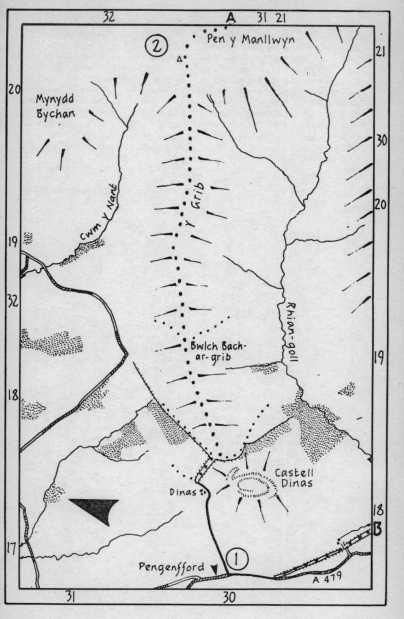

Mynydd Bychan

Pen y Manllwyn

②

Cwm y Nant

Y Grib

Rhian-goll

Bwlch Bach-
ar-grib

Castell
Dinas

Dinas

Pengenfford

①

A 479

2 From the cairn turn right and follow the path along the highest ground to the base of the old trig point on Waun Fach. Turn right and follow the clear path downhill past a cairn to Pen Trumau. Be sure to keep to the highest ground. After dropping very steeply down a narrow ridge, turn right at a cairn and follow a clear path which soon forks to the left to contour the flank of a hill.

3 On reaching a gate in a wire fence drop sharply downhill along an enclosed track to a road. Turn right and then left, pass the Cwm Fforest Riding Centre and where the road turns sharply back on itself, continue forward along a muddy enclosed track, cross a ford to reach the road and $\frac{1}{4}$ mile later, your car.

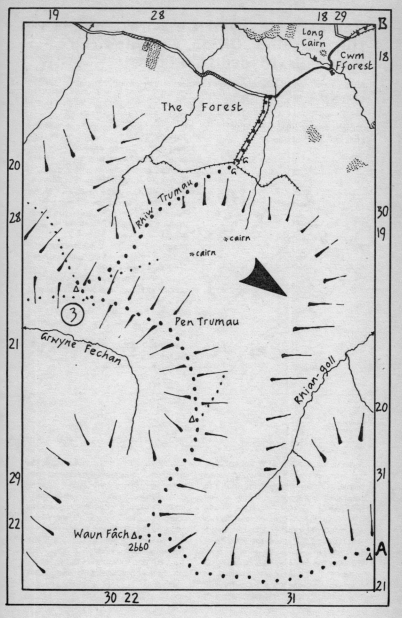

19   28   18 29   B

                                        Long
                                        Cairn
                                                Cwm
                                                Fforest   18

The   Forest

20
                                                            30
                        G   19
            Rhiw Trumau   G
                                    *cairn
                            *cairn
28

        △
    ③   Pen Trumau
21
arwyne Fechan
                        △   Rhian-goll   20

29   31

22
    Waun Fâch △
            2660   △ A
                                                            21
    30 22   31

Route 22. Mynydd Du Forest, Capel-y-ffin, Pen Rhos Dirion, Grwyne Fawr Reservoir, Mynydd Du Forest

A fairly easy route mostly following tracks across open country. There are splendid views across the Wye valley

Distance: 10½ miles
For: Walkers and riders

Terrain: Moderately difficult. (Much of the route follows clear tracks, but there is a ½-mile stretch from the edge of the forest to the top of the ridge where no proper path exists)
Route-finding: Moderately difficult. (Most of it is easy to follow along well-marked tracks, but there is a ½-mile stretch from the edge of the forest to the top of the ridge where no path exists)
Maps: 1:25000 Brecon Beacons Outdoor Leisure Map, Eastern Area; 1:50000 sheet 161
Start: The Forestry Commission car park at Yr Eithen near Blaen-y-cwm at the end of the road which follows the Grwyne Fawr valley about 10 miles north of Abergavenny, grid reference SN252287
Parking: Plentiful at start of the walk
Buses: None
Refreshments: None

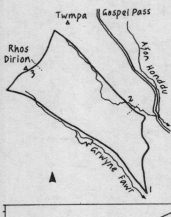

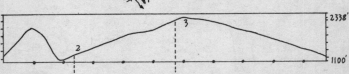

1 From the picnic area at Yr Eithen, walk upstream along the fence which marks the edge of the forest. Turn right into the forest at a gate and follow a clear path which bends to the right to join a forestry road. Turn left and follow the road until it makes a hairpin bend. After turning 90°, climb the steep bank on the left where there is a path through the forest which emerges on to open country at a gate. There is no path, so continue forward to the top of the ridge on a compass bearing of 353°. Cross the path which runs the length of the ridge at a cairn and then go down to the edge of the escarpment where there is another cairn. Follow the clear, steep track down the scarp. Do not cross the stile at the edge of the forest but turn left down the side of the fence to the Grange Trekking Centre and on to the road. Turn left and follow the road to where the metalling ceases at a bridge and ford.

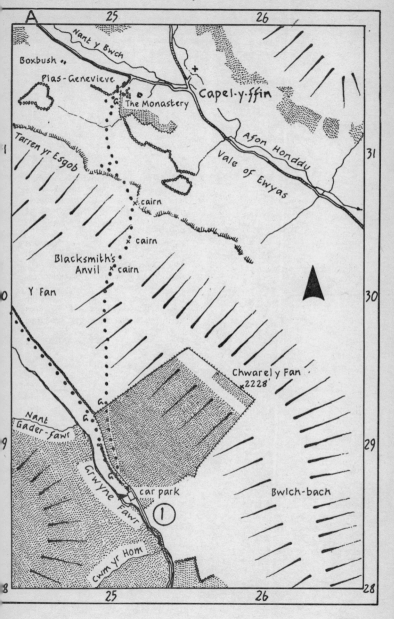

A

25   26

Nant y Bwch

Boxbush

Plas - Genevieve

The Monastery   Capel·y·ffin

1   31

Tarren yr Esgob   Afon Honddu

                          Vale of Ewyas

                    x cairn

                x cairn

Blacksmith's
Anvil   x cairn

Y Fan

                                    Chwarel y Fan
                                        ·2228

30

Nant
Gader-fawr

9   29

                    car park

Grwyne Fawr   ①   Bwlch-bach

                Cwm yr Hom

8   28
25   26

129

2 Continue forward along a track to a gate which leads on to open country. After ½ mile the track follows a stream and then continues on to a steep escarpment with splendid views over the Wye Valley. Turn left and follow the escarpment for 1 mile to reach a trig point.

Continued on p. 132

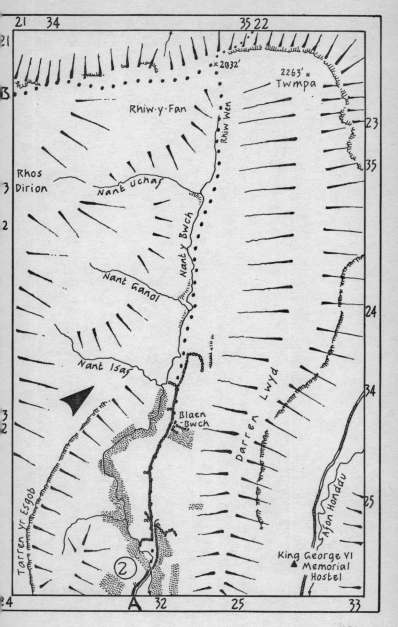

21   34   35 22

Rhiw·y·Fan

×2032'

2263' ×
Twmpa

Rhos
Dirion

Nant uchaf

Rhiw Wen

Nant y Bwch

Nant Ganol

Nant Isaf

Darren Lwyd

Blaen
Bwch

Tarren yr Esgob

②

Afon Honddu

King George VI
Memorial
Hostel

21   23

B   35

3   24

2

3   34
2

                                      25

24   A   32   25   33

3 About ½ mile beyond the trig point turn left along a broad path which runs past the Grwyne Fawr Reservoir to the car park at Yr Eithen.

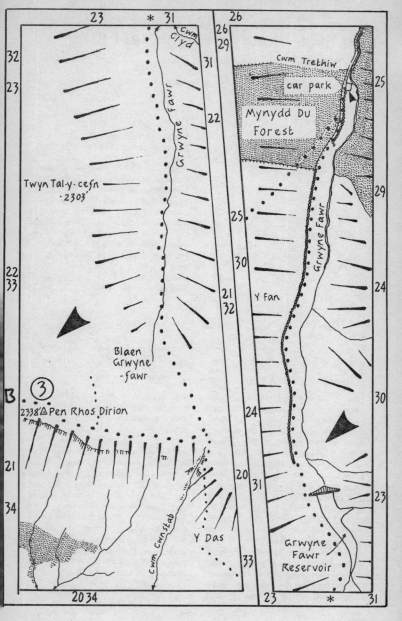

23   * 31
32
23
Cwm
Clyd
31
Grwyne Fawr
22
Twyn Tal-y-cefn
· 2303'
22
33
③
B
2338'△ Pen Rhos Dirion
21
34
Blaen
Grwyne
-fawr
Cwm Cwn stab
Y Das
20 34

26
26
29
Cwm Trethiw
car park
25
Mynydd Du
Forest
29
25
30
Y Fan
21
32
24
24
20
31
30
23
Grwyne
Fawr
Reservoir
23   *   31

Grwyne Fawr

Route 23. Mynydd Du Forest, Garn Wen, Bal-bach, Nant y Gwyddel, Bal-bach, Mynydd Du Forest

A figure-of-eight route mostly across open country offering fine views

Distance: 8 miles
For: Walkers only

Bal Bach

Terrain: Moderately difficult
Route-finding: Moderately difficult
Maps: 1:25000 Brecon Beacons Outdoor Leisure Map, Eastern Area; 1:50000 sheet 161
Start: The Forestry Commission car park at Pont Cadwgan about 7½ miles north of Abergavenny on the road which follows the Grwyne Fawr valley, grid reference SN257252
Parking: Plentiful at the start of the walk
Buses: None
Refreshments: None

1   Take the track which runs from the far corner of the car park to an enclosed track which runs below the abandoned farm at Cadwgan. On reaching open country at a gate by a stream continue forward, following the wall on the right which after a bit becomes a fence. At a junction of paths, move away from the fence and follow a broad track which meets a stone wall on the left. Where the wall ends, turn left and follow it for 50 yds to meet an enclosed track at a T-junction. Turn left and follow the track to reach open country at a gate. Continue forward along a grassy track which moves slightly away from the wall on the left. 100 yds later fork right along the lesser track, climb to the summit of Garn Wen to reach in about a mile the large cairn on Bal-bach. Ignore the path which crosses and continue forward to a white post and fork right.

After about a mile the path bears right   2
at a ruined building and drops steeply downhill. On reaching a gate in a wall *do not pass through the gate* but turn right and go downhill to reach another path. Turn right and follow the fence on the left for ½ mile to a gate and a stile which gives access to a stream and lane by a cottage. Continue forward along a sunken track which follows a wall. Fork right and climb uphill to reach the cairn at Bal-bach.

Continued on p. 136

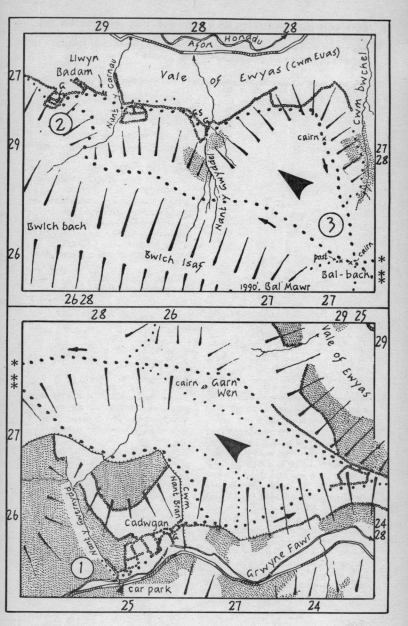

Vale of Ewyas (Cwm Ewas)

29   28   28

Afon Honddu

Llwyn Badam

Nant y Carnau

G.S.

Nant y Gader

cairn ×

Cwm bwchel

②

27

29

Bwlch bach

26

Bwlch Isaf

③

post ×··· cairn *

Bal-bach *

*

1990'. Bal Mawr

26 28   27   27

28   26   29 25

Vale of Ewyas

29

*
*
*

cairn ≫ Garn Wen

27

Nant y Gwryd

Nant Bran

Cwm

Cadwgan

26

①

car park

25   27   24

Grwyne Fawr

24
28

3 Continue forward aiming for the forest ahead and on reaching a track turn left and follow the forest edge. Where the forest ends, turn sharp right and follow the path downhill to meet a stone wall. Turn right, walk to the gate and retrace your steps past Cadwgan to the car park.

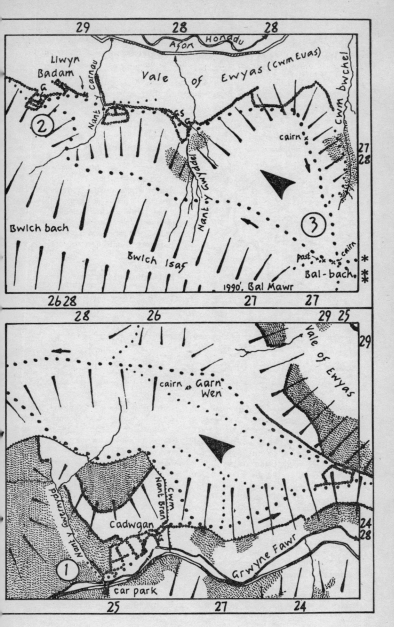

29   28   28

Afon Honddu

Llwyn Badam

Vale of Ewyas (Cwm Euas)

Nant y Carnau

Cwm bwchel

② cairn

Bwlch bach

Nant y Gwryddau

Bwlch Isaf

post ✕ cairn ✱
Bal-bach. ✱

③

1990', Bal Mawr

26 28   27   27

28   26   29 25

29

cairn Garn Wen

Vale of Ewyas

Nant y Grwyne ???

Nant Bran

Cwm

Cadwgan

Grwyne Fawr

24 28

①

car park

25   27   24

137

Route 24. Mynydd Du Forest, Disgwylfa, Blaenau, Draen, Crug Mawr, Mynydd Du Forest

A fine figure-of-eight route through forests and across open country mostly following clear tracks

Distance: 9½ miles
For: Walkers only

Terrain: Moderately difficult
Route-finding: Easy
Maps: 1:25000 Brecon Beacons Outdoor Leisure Map, Eastern Area; 1:50000 sheet 161
Start: The Forestry Commission car park at Pont Cadwgan, about 7½ miles north of Abergavenny on the road which follows the Grwyne Fawr valley, grid reference SN257252
Parking: Plentiful at the start of the walk
Buses: None
Refreshments: None

1 From the car park walk to the road and turn right. After about ¼ mile turn left along a broad gravelled track which starts to climb gently through the forest at an acute angle to the road. Keep to the main track round a hairpin bend and at the next junction of tracks keep forward. Just before reaching a farm, bear left and pass through some sheep pens and three gates very close together to reach a track. Continue forward and pass through a gap to where the track becomes enclosed and keep on to reach a gate which gives access to a Forestry Commission track. *Do not pass through this gate, but turn left, cross the stile and walk up an enclosed path alongside the forest edge.* Pass

through a gate and continue forward for 100 yds to a gravelled Forestry Commission track. Turn left and follow this wide track for 600 yds to a point where it bears left. Fork right here and follow a narrower but still very obvious stony track. On reaching a wide gravelled track, cross over, continue forward and after a short distance you will reach a gate at the edge of the forest near the top of the ridge. Continue forward following a clear track to reach in 100 yds or so a track running along the top of the ridge. Turn left and follow this for about ½ mile until opposite a gate in the forest on the left.

At this point turn right (there is no

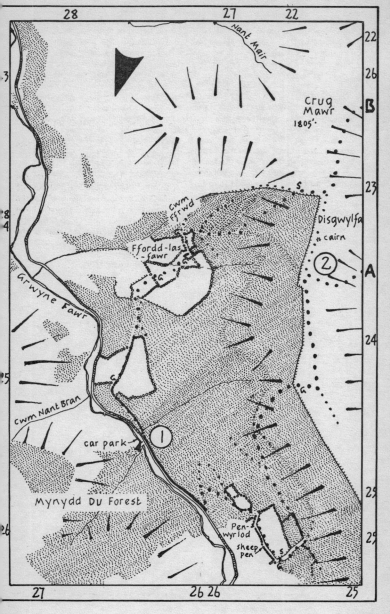

Nant Mair

Crug
Mawr
1805'.

B

Cwm
Ffrwd

S

Disgwylfa

cairn

Ffordd-las
-fawr

G

G

②

A

Grwyne Fawr

G

C

Cwm Nant Bran

car park

①

Mynydd Du Forest

Pen-
wyrlod

sheep
pen

S

path) and walk through the heather for 200 yds or so until you are looking down into an attractive cwm. Continue forward until reaching a path which appears to contour the cwm. (*Now turn to p. 142*.)

(*Continued from p. 142*) On top of the ridge, take the right-hand fork and walk towards the forest. At the corner of the forest, turn right and walk steeply downhill towards the valley bottom keeping the edge of the forest on the left. After 200 yds, turn left over a stile and follow a gravelled road for about 300 yds. Where the road bears sharp left, turn right and walk steeply downhill through the trees. Cross another gravelled track and continue forward downhill to reach another track. Turn left and pass through a gate to reach in a short distance an old farm. Turn right and pass through the farm buildings and then follow a clear path which bears left across a field and over a tiny stream and then turns right and becomes enclosed. Follow the enclosed track until reaching a major junction of paths in the forest. Fork right and continue to the road and the car park opposite.

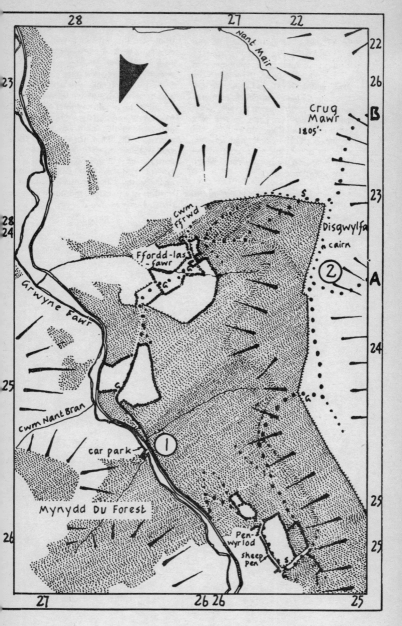

Turn left and follow this path downhill as it gradually moves towards the stream in the cwm and then passes through a gate and becomes an enclosed track. Follow the track to the road at Blaenau. Turn left and follow this country lane (which carries hardly any traffic) for about a mile. After passing Llwyn-on Farm on the right continue for another hundred yards or so along the road and then turn left through a gate by an animal shelter and enter an enclosed track which goes off at an angle.

3 Follow the track to the old farmhouse at Draen, enter the farmyard and high up on the right you will see a gate behind the farmhouse that is almost level with the roof. Pass through this gate and walk uphill with a wall on your right and almost immediately pass through another gate. Ignore the first path which comes in from the left and continue to follow the wall until reaching a gate at the forest edge. *Do not pass through this gate* but turn left and take the clear path which follows a wall on the edge of the forest. The wall bears round sharply right and the path leaves it at this point and joins it later on, and then, 250 yds later, bears away to the left and makes towards the top of the ridge. Ignore all minor paths. (*Now turn to p. 140.*)

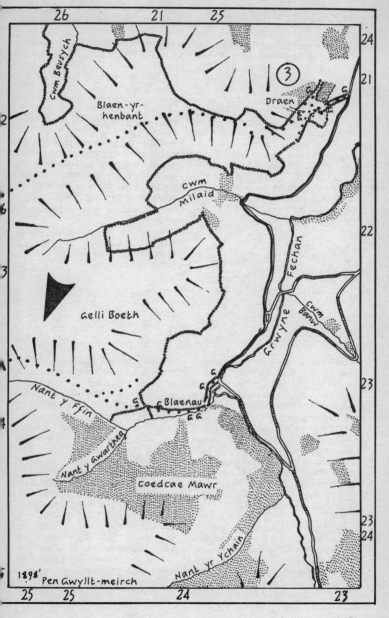

26   21   25

24

21

Cwm Bewsych

③

Draen

Blaen-yr-henbant

2

cwm
Milaid

16

22

3

Gelli Boeth

cwm
Banw

Grwyne Fechan

23

Nant y Ffin

Blaenau

7

Nant y Gwartheg

Coedcae Mawr

23

23
24

1898' Pen Gwyllt-meirch

Nant yr Ychain

25   25   24   23

143

Route 25. The Sugar Loaf, Abergavenny

A popular route through forests and across open country on well-marked tracks. In fine weather, suitable for fit novices

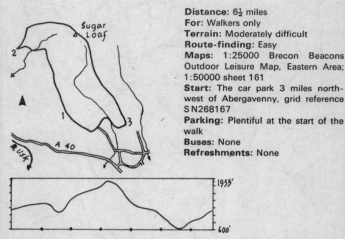

Distance: 6½ miles
For: Walkers only
Terrain: Moderately difficult
Route-finding: Easy
Maps: 1:25000 Brecon Beacons Outdoor Leisure Map, Eastern Area; 1:50000 sheet 161
Start: The car park 3 miles north-west of Abergavenny, grid reference SN268167
Parking: Plentiful at the start of the walk
Buses: None
Refreshments: None

1 Leave the car park, following the sign-posted route near the National Trust collecting box. Head northwards and at the top of the slope where the Sugar Loaf comes into view fork left and follow the wall. 200 yds later fork right and leave the wall to follow a broad path through the bracken and then an earth bank. Instead of taking the path which leads directly to the Sugar Loaf, turn left and head downhill away from the mountain. 100 yds later fork right and drop steeply downhill to the valley bottom near the forest.

2 Jump across the narrow stream and follow the obvious track uphill. Here there are a number of paths and tracks. Follow the path that leads up the ridge and then, just below some trees, aim for some stunted trees and a wall. (In summer the wall may be obscured by

bracken.) Rounding a bend where the whole valley comes into view there are two gates on the left. Turn right here and follow a broad path that leads towards the Sugar Loaf. At the top of the ridge turn right at a T-junction of paths and follow the clearly defined path along the ridge to just below the summit of the Sugar Loaf. Bear right and follow the path which climbs up to the trig point. Look towards Abergavenny and note the clear path which follows the top of the ridge. Take this path and on reaching a major junction of paths with a wire fence and gate about 50 yds on the left, continue on for 50 yds and then fork left to follow the wire fence and wall on the left. Where the path drops steeply downhill fork right to arrive at a lane near a National Trust sign.

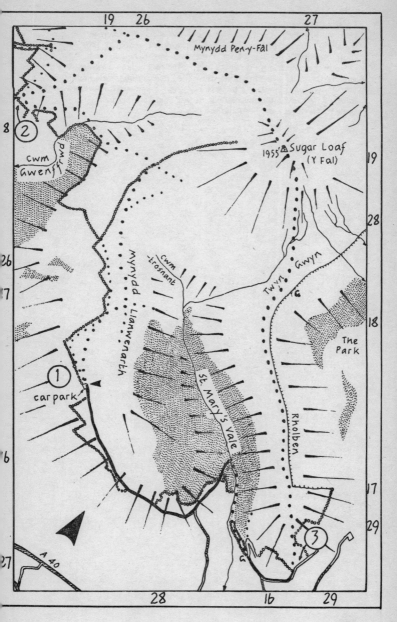

Mynydd Pen-y-Fal

1955 △ Sugar Loaf
(Y Fal)

Cwm Gwenff

Cwm trosnant

Mynydd Llanwenarth

Twyn Gwyn

The Park

St. Mary's Vale

Rholben

car park

A 40

3   Follow the lane downhill to a T-junction and turn right. Continue until the metalling ends at St Mary's Vale and a footpath sign 'To the Sugar Loaf'. Pass through the gate and go downhill to a stream. Cross it by a footbridge, turn left immediately, climb the bank and follow a narrow path uphill. 30 yds to the left is a stone wall. Pass through a gap in a line of trees and continue forward uphill to reach a gate at a roughly metalled lane midway between two cottages. Turn left and follow the lane. On reaching the road junction turn right, immediately fork right again and follow the signs for the Sugar Loaf car park.

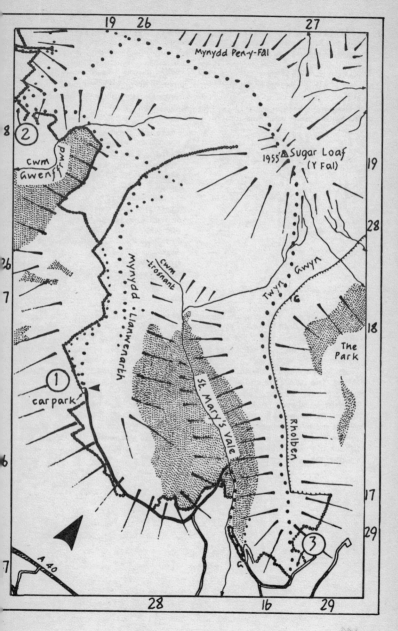

19 26   27

Mynydd Pen-y-Fal

8
②
Cwm
Gwenffrwd

1955 △ Sugar Loaf
(Y Fal)

19

28

26

7

Mynydd Llanwenarth
Cwm Trosnant

Twyn Gwyn
TG

18

The Park

①
carpark

St. Mary's Vale

Rholben

17

29

③

7
A 40

28   16   29

147

Route 26. Ysgyryd Fawr, near Abergavenny

A popular route rising to 1,600 ft. In fine weather it gives the opportunity for strollers to get the feel of a mountain-in-miniature in perfect safety

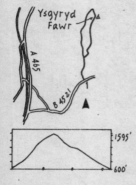

Distance: 3 miles
For: Walkers only
Terrain: Easy
Route-finding: Easy
Maps: 1:25000 Brecon Beacons Outdoor Leisure Map, Eastern Area; 1:50000 sheet 161
Start: The car park 3½ miles northeast of Abergavenny on the B4521, grid reference SN328165
Parking: Plentiful at the start of the walk
Buses: None
Refreshments: None

1 From the car park walk downhill along the road for about 50 yds to a footpath sign and stile on the right. Before reaching the top of the field, at the corner of the wood, turn right and cross a waymarked stile into Skirrid Wood. The path climbs quite steeply using a series of steps, and emerges from the wood at a stile. Turn right and follow the stone wall on the right. Where the path divides, fork right and follow the wall and a wire fence. Where the path divides again turn sharply left and climb to the very obvious summit, ignoring a path running off to the left. Continue ahead to the trig point and then bear left to reach some rocky boulders where the path descends very steeply. About 100 yds before reaching the woodland, turn left along a broad path. After nearly a mile the path runs beside a wall which should be followed, ignoring all paths which branch off, to the stile which leads into Skirrid Wood. Turn into the wood and retrace the original route to the car park.

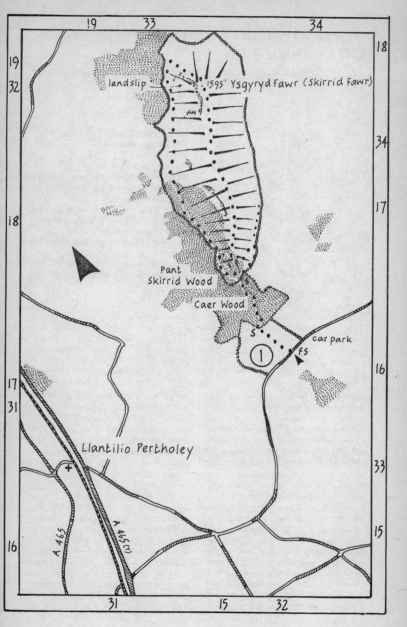

landslip

1595' Ysgyryd Fawr (Skirrid Fawr)

Pant
Skirrid Wood

Caer Wood

S

car park

FS

①

Llantilio Pertholey

A 465

A 465 (T)

Route 27. Llanthony, The Vale of Ewyas, Offa's Dyke Path

An easy route which includes a short but fine ridge walk along Offa's Dyke Path

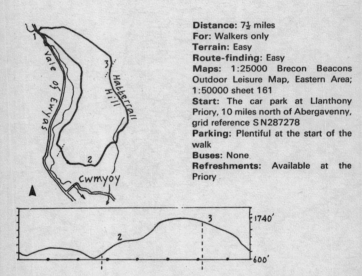

Distance: 7½ miles
For: Walkers only
Terrain: Easy
Route-finding: Easy
Maps: 1:25000 Brecon Beacons Outdoor Leisure Map, Eastern Area; 1:50000 sheet 161
Start: The car park at Llanthony Priory, 10 miles north of Abergavenny, grid reference SN287278
Parking: Plentiful at the start of the walk
Buses: None
Refreshments: Available at the Priory

1 From the car park return to the road and turn left. Follow the road for about 250 yds until it turns sharp right. Pass through the gate on the left and follow a clear path to two gates on the opposite side of the field. Pass through the lower gate and follow the left-hand headland to reach a stile. Cross it, and go over the field, parallel to the left-hand headland. At a barbed-wire fence with no access through it, turn left and walk to the top of the field where a gate gives access to a farm track going down to another gate. Pass through this, and follow the right-hand headland until the track turns sharp right. Here there are two gates. Take the left-hand gate and walk down the right-hand headland to a farm. Pass through the farmyard, which has a metalled lane through it, and pass through a series of gates to the other side of the farmyard. Where the metalled lane turns sharp right strike leftwards, following the left-hand headland of the field to reach a gate. Pass through and continue forward to a gate and a gap. *Do not pass through the gap* but take the gate on the right and follow the left-hand headland of that field to a stile. Cross it, and follow the path across the field to a gap in a belt of trees with a stream through it. Continue on to another gap and so to a gate and a stream giving access to a ruined farmyard. Pass through the gate and immediately take the gate on the right into the farmyard. Follow the path to a gate in a fence and continue to a gap and on to

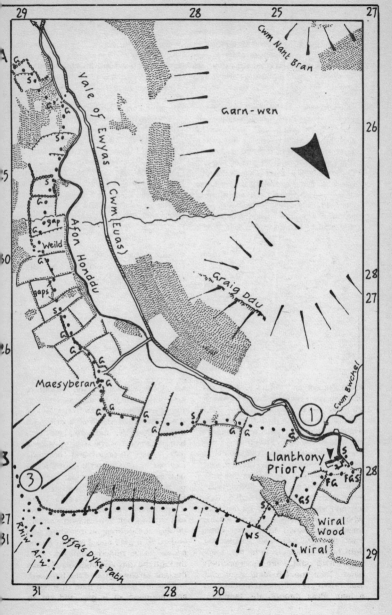

29 28 25 27

A

Cwm Nant Bran

Garn-wen

26

Vale of Ewyas (Cwm Euas)

Afon Honddu

gap

Weild

28
27

gaps

Graig Ddu

Maesyberan

Cwm Bwchel

① 1

26

28

③ 3

Llanthony Priory

27
31

Rhiw Arw

Offa's Dyke Path

Wiral Wood

Wiral

29

31 28 30

another gate. Pass through it, and go down the field to the far right-hand corner to a stile and on to another in the fence ahead. Continue to the river bank. *Do not cross the bridge* but pass through a waymarked gate and go up the hill on a clear track. At the top of the hill the track appears to end at a barbed-wire fence. Here, turn left and walk uphill for about 30 yds to a stile on the right. Cross it, and follow the left-hand headland to the upper of two gates which give access to a farm. (*Now turn to p. 154.*)

3   (*Continued from p. 154*) At the far end of the ridge fork left and walk down to a stone wall from where Llanthony can be seen in the valley. Follow the clearly defined path until reaching a waymarked stile on the left. Cross the stile and walk down the left-hand headland following a wire fence to a waymarked stile at the bottom of the field. Cross the stile and turn right along a woodland track which runs downhill to a gate and a stile. Cross the stile and make for the gate clearly visible in the bottom left-hand corner of the field near the Priory. Cross the stile next to the gate at the footpath sign and follow the left-hand wall of the Priory until reaching a gate at the end of the field. Cross the stile next to the gate at a footpath sign, turn left and walk down the lane for a few yards to a stile on the left. Cross the stile and walk to the car park ahead.

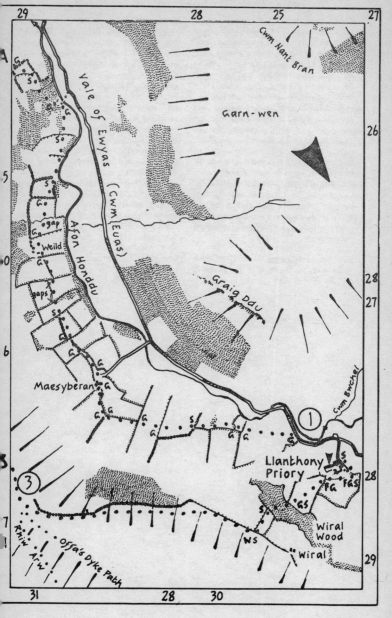

Cwm Nant Bran

Garn-wen

Vale of Ewyas (Cwm Ewas)

Afon Honddu

29 28 25 27

26

gap

Weild

gaps

Graig Ddu

Maesyberan

Llanthony Priory

FG FAS

GS

Wiral Wood

Wiral

WS

Cwm Bwchel

Offa's Dyke Path

Rhiw Arw

31 28 30

28

27

6

7

28

29

①

③

Pass through the farmyard to reach another house with a lawn in front of it. Cross this to reach another gate and continue along a clearly defined track to a waymarked gate and a stile. About 300 yds later fork left and go uphill for a short distance. Turn sharp right at a T-junction and walk down this well-defined path with a ruined wall on the right to a gate. Pass through the gate and cross a stream. At this point the path apparently bears sharp right to a gate. *Do not bear right* but instead turn left and walk uphill to an overgrown track which emerges after 200 yds at a gate by a ruined building. Continue uphill on a well-defined path following the wall and at the top of a col there are two kissing gates and a stile which give access into a walled grassy path.

2   Turn left, walk along the lane until the walls end, turn right and go downhill following the wall on the right to a gate. Pass through the gate and continue to another where a track comes in from the right. Pass through the gate and continue past a farm to a stile in a fence. Cross the stile and continue forward to where the fence on the right ends. Continue forward, bearing slightly right to cross a stile and stream. Continue forward up a steep hill to reach a broad grassy track. Turn left along the track which sweeps round to the right and climbs to a gate. Pass through the gate and follow the grassy track as it curves sharply left. At this point the path peters out into a number of sheep tracks, so make for a rocky outcrop which is the remains of an old quarry. Turn right and head eastwards to the top of the ridge and onto the very broad Offa's Dyke Path. Turn left and follow the path for a mile and cross a narrow ridge with good views into the valleys on either side.

(*Continued on p. 152.*)

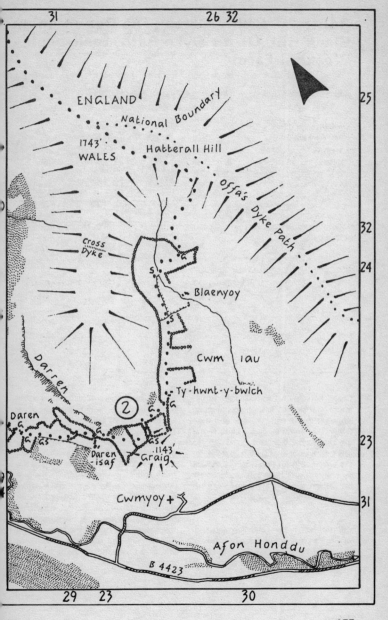

ENGLAND

National Boundary

WALES

1743'

Hatterall Hill

Offa's Dyke Path

Cross
Dyke

Blaenyoy

Cwm Iau

Ty-hwnt-y-bwlch

Darren

Daren

Daren
isaf

.1143'
Graig

Cwmyoy +

Afon Honddu

B 4423

31   26 32

25

32

24

23

31

29 23   30

155

Route 28. Crib y Garth (The Cat's Back), Black Hill, Offa's Dyke Path, Beili-bach, Blackhill Farm

A fine high-level route which included a short stretch of Offa's Dyke Path

Distance: 8 miles
For: Walkers only

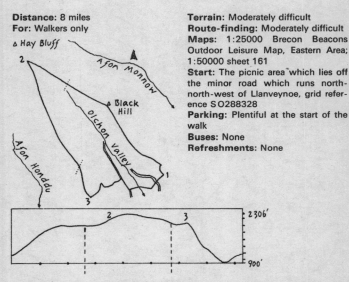

Terrain: Moderately difficult
Route-finding: Moderately difficult
Maps: 1:25000 Brecon Beacons Outdoor Leisure Map, Eastern Area; 1:50000 sheet 161
Start: The picnic area which lies off the minor road which runs north-north-west of Llanveynoe, grid reference S O288328
Parking: Plentiful at the start of the walk
Buses: None
Refreshments: None

1 Cross the stile and, ignoring the broad track, bear slightly left, climb the steep slope up to the narrow ridge and then follow it all the way past a cairn to the trig point on Black Hill (2,101 ft). At this point, bear slightly left and follow the broad path for about a mile. Where the path forks, bear left and shortly turn sharp left and climb the path up the hill. (*Continued on p. 158*.)

3 (*Continued from p. 158*) Turn left and follow the path, which soon becomes a track, and zig-zags down the hillside. At a junction of paths follow the one which leads towards a gate near the road. Turn right and follow the road to the second building on the left (Beili-bach), turn left and follow a track which passes the farm to reach a gate. Continue forward down the hill to a footbridge and then follow the track which goes half right up the hill. After a short distance the track peters out, but continue forward until reaching Blackhill Farm, which is hidden among trees. At the farm, cross the stream and follow the track up the hill to reach the road at a gate. Turn left, and then, shortly, right to return to the picnic area.

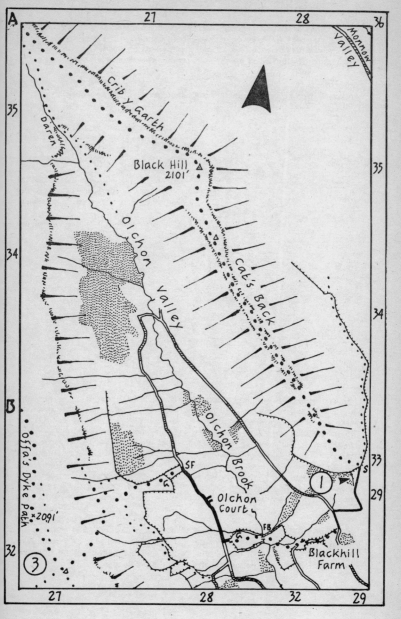

A 27 28 36

Monnow Valley

Crib y Garth

35

35

Daren

Black Hill
2101'

Olchon Valley

34

Cat's Back

34

B

Olchon Brook

Offa's Dyke Path

SF

G

x 2091'

Olchon Court

①

S

33

29

FB

G

32

③

Blackhill Farm

27 28 32 29

2 Follow Offa's Dyke Path along the ridge for 2½ miles until reaching the fourth cairn, where a path crosses. The correct cairn can further be identified because you should now be almost exactly opposite the road which runs up towards the picnic site on the hill on the other side of the valley.

(*Continued on p. 156.*)

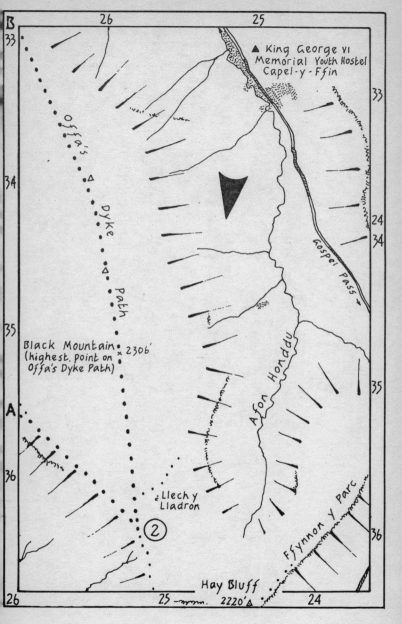

B

33

26   25

▲ King George VI
Memorial Youth Hostel
Capel-y-Ffin

33

Offa's

34

Dyke

24

34

Gospel Pass

Path

35

Black Mountain
(highest point on
Offa's Dyke Path)

× 2306'

Afon Honddu

35

A

36

Llech y
Lladron

②

Ffynnon y Parc

36

26   25 —ᴡᴡᴡ— 2220'△   Hay Bluff   24

Index of Place Names

Index of Place Names

Index of Place Names

The Penguin Footpath Guides

H. D. Westacott
Mapped by Hugh Richards

The Cornwall South Coast Path
Dartmoor for Walkers and Riders
The Devon South Coast Path
The Dorset Coast Path
The North Downs Way
The Ridgeway Path
The Somerset and North Devon Coast Path
The South Downs Way

also by H. D. Westacott in Penguins

The Walker's Handbook
Second Enlarged Edition

Maps, tents, clothes, rights of way, National Parks, the law,
hostels, farmers, gamekeepers, shoes, boots, safety and first
aid – all you need to know to walk safely and happily,
whether you take the low road or the high road. This new and
enlarged edition also includes extra chapters on challenge
walks and walking abroad.

More Penguins for Walkers

First Aid for Hill Walkers and Climbers
Jane Renouf and Stewart Hulse

This practical, sensible and long-needed manual will slip easily into a pocket or rucksack. It has been compiled with the aid of rescuers and experienced climbers and walkers from all over Britain. While not intended as a substitute for a first-aid course, it tells you how to deal with accidents on the mountainside and how to set about getting help in the most efficient and least panicky way: and, for easy reference, the authors list the different accidents and illnesses in alphabetical order, ranging from asthma to vertigo.

A Hitch-Hiker's Guide to Great Britain
Ken Lussey

Illustrated by Reg Piggott

Whether you're a beginner or an expert, this handbook provides the essential information to enable you to hitch safely and enjoyably from A to B, with the minimum of time, trouble and expense. Dividing Britain into ten regions for easy reference, the guide features

● maps show the best pick-up points on motorway junctions and A roads, rated according to a carefully devised grading system
● large-scale maps giving hitching-ratings at spots in city and town centres throughout Britain
● information on equipment, motorways and camping, and many more useful hints

A Choice of Penguins

The Penguin Guide to Prehistoric England and Wales
James Dyer

'An excellent guide . . . an essential companion' – *British Book News*

From Stonehenge and Silbury Hill to the magnificent cliff castles of Cornwall and the hill forts on the Welsh Marches, this Penguin guide covers, county by county, almost a thousand prehistoric sites in England and Wales.

Illustrated with plans, maps and photographs and including newly published information on recent excavations and discoveries, this guide will be of interest whether you enjoy history or archeology, or simply exploring the countryside.

The Town Gardener's Companion
Felicity Bryan

Former gardening columnist for the *Evening Standard*, Felicity Bryan has marshalled all her expertise and inventiveness in this month-by-month guide which includes sixteen pages of colour photographs. Here she demonstrates that lack of space offers a challenge of its own, and with ingenious planning the town gardener can produce a riot of flowers, foliage and vegetables the whole year round.

'An inspiring new book . . . a fertile source of ideas for turning a cat-ridden concrete backyard into a jungle of soothing green' – *Sunday Times*

A Choice of Penguin Handbooks

Buying a House or Flat
Second Edition
L. E. Vickers

Previously published as *Buying a House*, *Buying a House or Flat* is a concise, comprehensive and up-to-date account of how to acquire your own property.

All the details required are here – the financial and the legal, the building societies, the estate agents, solicitors and surveyors. Methodically Mrs Vickers outlines the various ways of raising money and the intricacies of conveyance and explains the force (or weakness) of a deposit, the meaning of 'freehold' and 'leasehold' and the rights of sitting tenants. On a less legal level she urges caution about the winter aspect of houses viewed in summer and other pitfalls, and reminds purchasers of all the arrangements to be made for moving day.

Those embarking on the exciting process of acquiring a new home could have no better guide: for the author, as well as having a sense of humour, has a flourishing practice as a solicitor.

Self Help House Repairs Manual
New Expanded Edition
Andrew Ingham

This updated and revised edition covers all aspects of basic repairs: electricity – repairing existing installations, putting in a new circuit; water – piping, sinks, baths, lavatories; gas – water heaters, cookers, fires; general repair – roofs, dry rot, plastering. New information on general carpentry, window repairs, draught-proofing, sanding floors and much more.

Games and Sports in Penguin Handbooks

The Game of Chess

H. Golombek

'A lucid and logical introduction to the game . . . sound instruction all the way through' – *The Times Literary Supplement*

Photography

Eric de Maré

Sixth edition

Designed to help and stimulate the amateur photographer, this book gives a straightforward account of the craft of photography in all its aspects.

Sailing

Peter Heaton

Fifth edition

This profusely illustrated handbook caters for the beginner, whether he wants to buy, fit out and sail a yacht or just read the sea-lore and learn the shanties.

The Penguin Book of Squash

Samir Nadim

This is a book for absolute beginners and for people who want to improve their game. Samir Nadim hopes that by following his step-by-step approach more people will play squash, and play it well.